THE

ROYAL

POCK

1994/95

Editor - Charles Heyman

Copyright © R & F (Defence Publications) 1994

First Edition 1994
ISBN 0 85052 416 4

Price £3.95 (Mail Order £4.75 including post & packing.)
There are special rates for purchases of more then 10 books
From: Pen & Sword Books Ltd
47 Church Street
Barnsley
S70 2AS
Telephone: 0226 734222   Fax: 0226 734438

The information in this publication has been gathered from
unclassified sources.

Front Cover: A Tornado GR1 of No 9 Sqn carrying 3 x ALARM missiles.
Rear Cover: Ground crews servicing aircraft at RAF St Athan.

LEO COOPER
LONDON

THE ROYAL AIR FORCE

This publication arrives on the market at a difficult time for the Royal Air Force. Decisions are being made now that will directly affect the RAF's ability to both defend the airspace of the United Kingdom, and provide the required strategic support for the period 2010 and beyond. In an era of shrinking defence budgets and political uncertainty, neither the Air Staff nor the politicians charged with making decisions regarding future procurement are to be envied.

It is worth reminding ourselves that in almost every major conflict since the 1930s ground operations have not been successful until the air force of one side has either been destroyed or significantly reduced. In some cases the outcome of the conflict has been decided within the first 30 minutes, and an air force destroyed on the ground, or destroyed in the air, because of the lack of a technological edge is a massive financial investment totally wasted.

A modern air force cannot be stood down - the air defence radars must be active 24 hours a day and interceptors ready at a moments notice. In a period of reduced tension, operational readiness can be reduced, but threats have a nasty habit of being cyclical. Unfortunately history tells us that a reduced threat today, generally means an increased threat tomorrow, and air forces do not get second chances. Air forces are never offered "Dunkirk" type miracles, whereby they retire to their home base to retrain and refit. A nation makes its investment and future security is decided.

Aircraft designs have long lead times, the first prototype Tornado flew in 1974 - twenty years ago, and procurement decisions taken now will have a great effect on our children's security. It is not our function to "beat a drum" for any particular system. All we ask is that the importance of the procurement decisions being taken now be realised by all concerned; that the defence planners remember that every penny of the defence budget is important - inter-service rivalry is a dead-end; and that the politicians understand the gravity of the decisions that must finally be theirs.

At 6pm on the 17th August 1940, the Operations Officer at HQ Fighter Command marked up 276 Spitfires, and about double that number of older, less capable Hurricanes, as being serviceable for the following day's operations. The enemy had three massive air fleets with over 2,000 aircraft available. In it's "History Account" at the "Bank of Miracles" the United Kingdom is probably overdrawn.

CONTENTS

CHAPTER 1 - USEFUL INFORMATION

UK Statistics

Population - 56,696,600

Population Strengths for Military Analysis:

Age Group:	13-17	18-22	23-32
Men	1,833,500	2,041,800	4,430,600
Women	1,744,300	1,942,300	4,253,900

Government:

The executive government is vested nominally in the Crown, but for practical purposes in a committee of Ministers known as the Cabinet. For the implementation of policy, the Cabinet is dependent upon the support of a majority of the Members of Parliament in the House of Commons. The head of the ministry and leader of the Cabinet is the Prime Minister. Within the Cabinet, defence matters are the responsibility of the Secretary of State for Defence.

Total British Armed Forces (as at 1 October 1993)

Regular: 266,500; Locally Entered 8,167; Regular Reserves 261,700; Volunteer Reserves 81,700; Cadet Forces 137,500; MOD Civilians 145,700.

Regular Army 130,873; Royal Navy 57,720; Royal Air Force 77,986; (Note: Royal Naval figure includes some 7,000 Royal Marines and the Air Force figure some 3,000 RAF Regiment personnel.

Strategic Forces: 32 Polaris missiles in 2 submarines - plus 1 submarine in extended refit.

Navy: 57,720 - Reducing to 52,500: 18 x Submarines; 3 x Aircraft Carriers; 40 x Destroyers and Frigates; 30 x Mine Counter Measures Vessels; 35 x Patrol Craft; 4 x Harrier Squadrons; 13 x Helicopter Squadrons; 3 x Commando Groups: Royal Fleet Auxiliary - 3 x Large Fleet Tankers; 3 x Small Fleet Tankers; 3 x Support Tankers; 4 x Fleet Replenishment Ships; 1 x Helicopter Support Ship; 5 x Landing Ships; 1 x Forward Repair Ship.

Merchant Naval Vessels Registered in the UK: 384 x Offshore Support & Fishing Vessels; 34 x Tankers; 91 x General Cargo Vessels; 3 x Cruise Ships; 46 x Roll on - Roll off Ferries; 58 x Tugs. (Note: There are 47 x Tankers and 14 x General Cargo Vessels registered in overseas Crown Territories).

Army: 130,873 (including some 6,000 Gurkhas) - Reducing to 119,000; 1 x Corps

Headquarters in Germany; 1 x Armoured Division in Germany; 1 x Division in UK; 4 x Brigade Headquarters in Germany; 18 x Brigade Headquarters in UK; 1 x Airborne Brigade in UK; 1 x Gurkha Infantry Bde in Hong Kong; 1 x Infantry Bde in Berlin - withdrawing in 1995. To reduce to 116,000 by 1995.

Air Force: 77,986 - Reducing to 70,000; 6 x Strike/Attack Squadrons; 5 x Offensive Support Squadrons; 6 x Air Defence Squadrons; 3 x Maritime Patrol Squadrons; 5 x Reconnaissance Squadrons; 1 x Airborne Early Warning Squadron; 13 x Transport Squadrons; 3 x Tanker Squadrons; 2 x Search and Rescue Squadrons; 1 x EW Training/Radar Calibration Squadron; 1 x Target Towing Squadron; 5 x Surface to Air Missile Squadrons; 4 x Ground Defence Squadrons.

Royal Air Force Equipment Summary

Aircraft available for immediate operations as at 1 January 1993 - we estimate some 560 combat aircraft capable of delivering missiles or ordnance.

133 x Tornado GR1; 26 x Tornado GR1A; 127 x Tornado F3; 57 x Harrier; 124 x Hawk; 43 x Jaguar GR1A; 16 x Jaguar T2A; 3 x Nimrod R1; 36 x Nimrod MR2; 7 x E-3D Sentry; 16 x Canberra; 9 x VC10 K2/K3; 10 x VC10 C1/C1K; 9 x Tristar K1/KC1/C2; 58 x Hercules; 12 x HS125; 3 x BAe 146; 6 x Andover; 60 x Chipmunk; 120 x Bulldog; 126 x Tucano; 18 x Dominie; 11 x Jetstream; 28 x Gazelle; 26 x Chinook; 19 x Sea King; 54 x Wessex; 37 x Puma.

Squadron Listing (As at 1 April 1994)

1 Sqn	14 x Harrier	RAF Wittering
2 Sqn	13 x Tornado GR1A	RAF Marham
3 Sqn	13 x Harrier	RAF Laarbruch
4 Sqn	13 x Harrier	RAF Laarbruch
5 Sqn	13 x Tornado F3	RAF Coningsby
6 Sqn	14 x Jaguar	RAF Coltishall
7 Sqn	18 x Chinook; 1 x Gazelle	RAF Odiham
8 Sqn	7 x E-3D Sentry	RAF Waddington
9 Sqn	13 x Tornado GR1	RAF Bruggen
10 Sqn	10 x VC10 C1/C1K	RAF Brize Norton
11 Sqn	13 x Tornado F3	RAF Leeming
12 Sqn	13 x Tornado GR1B	RAF Lossiemouth
13 Sqn	13 x Tornado GR1A	RAF Marham
14 Sqn	13 x Tornado GR1	RAF Bruggen
15 Sqn (R)	25 x Tornado GR1	RAF Lossiemouth
16 Sqn (R)	10 x Jaguar	RAF Lossiemouth
17 Sqn	13 x Tornado GR1	RAF Bruggen
18 Sqn	5 x Chinook; 5 x Puma	RAF Laarbruch
19 Sqn (R)	25 x Hawk	RAF Chivenor
20 Sqn (R)	16 x Harrier (approx)	RAF Wittering

6

Squadron	Aircraft	Base
22 Sqn	11 x Wessex	RAF Chivenor (1)
24 Sqn	13 x Hercules C1/C3/C1K	RAF Lyneham
25 Sqn	13 x Tornado F3	RAF Leeming
27 Sqn (R)	4 x Chinook HC1/5 x Puma	RAF Odiham
29 Sqn	13 x Tornado F3	RAF Coningsby
30 Sqn	13 x Hercules C1/C3/C1K	RAF Lyneham
31 Sqn	13 x Tornado GR1	RAF Bruggen
32 Sqn	12 x HS125; 2 x Andover 4 x Gazelle	RAF Northolt
33 Sqn	12 x Puma	RAF Odiham
39 Sqn (1 PRU)	7 x Canberra	RAF Marham
41 Sqn	14 x Jaguar	RAF Coltishall
42 Sqn (R)	5 x Nimrod MR2	RAF Kinloss
43 Sqn	16 x Tornado F3	RAF Leuchars
45 Sqn (R)	11 x Jetstream	RAF Finningley
47 Sqn	11 x Hercules C1/C3	RAF Lyneham
51 Sqn	3 x Nimrod R1	RAF Wyton (Waddington 1995)
54 Sqn	15 x Jaguar	RAF Coltishall
55 Sqn (R)	VC-10/Tristar	RAF Brize Norton
56 Sqn (R)	24 x Tornado F3	RAF Coningsby
57 Sqn (R)	5 x Hercules	RAF Lyneham
60 Sqn	9 x Wessex	RAF Benson
70 Sqn	12 x Hercules	RAF Lyneham
72 Sqn	15 x Wessex	RAF Aldergrove
74 Sqn (R)	21 x Hawk	RAF Valley
92 Sqn (R)	22 x Hawk	RAF Chivenor
100 Sqn	12 x Hawks	RAF Finningley
101 Sqn	9 x VC10 K2/K3	RAF Brize Norton
111 Sqn	16 x Tornado F3	RAF Leuchars
120 Sqn	7 x Nimrod MR2	RAF Kinloss (3)
201 Sqn	7 x Nimrod MR2	RAF Kinloss
202 Sqn	15 x Sea King	RAF Boulmer (4)
206 Sqn	7 x Nimrod MR2	RAF Kinloss
216 Sqn	9 x Tristar K1/KC1/C2	RAF Brize Norton
230 Sqn	15 x Puma	RAF Aldergrove
234 Sqn (R)	20 x Hawk	RAF Valley (4)
360 Sqn	10 x Canberra	RAF Wyton (Disbands 10/94)
617 Sqn	13 x Tornado GR1	RAF Lossiemouth (from 4/94)

Notes

(1) 22 Squadron has detachments at Valley and Chivenor.

(2) 115 Sqn is to be contractorised and the aircraft will be transferred to the Hunting Aviation's base at East Midlands Airport. Once civilian crews have been trained 115 Sqn and the Andover Conversion Flight will disband.

(3) There are believed to be 26 x Nimrod MR2 at RAF Kinloss. For ease of accounting, we have shown the three operational squadrons with 7 aircraft and the

OCU - 42 Sqn (R) with 5.

(4) 202 Sqn has detachments at Leconfield, Lossiemouth, & Wattisham.

(5) 234 Sqn (R) becomes 208 Sqn (R) in 4/94.

(6) OCUs are being given Reserve Squadron numbers. For example the Nimrod OCU at RAF Kinloss will be known as 42 (Reserve) Sqn.

Units Outside UK/Germany

28 Sqn	8 x Wessex	Hong Kong	Sek Kong
84 Sqn	5 x Wessex	Cyprus	Akrotiri
78 Sqn	Chinook/Sea King	Falklands	Mount Pleasant
1312 Flight	Hercules	Falklands	Mount Pleasant
1435 Flight	Tornado F3	Falklands	Mount Pleasant
1563 Flight	Puma (1)	Belize	International Airport

Notes

(1) Units in Belize will withdraw in late 1993/early 1994.

(2) There are RAF flying units deployed in the Arabian Gulf (Op Jural) and Turkey (Op Warden) in support of United Nations operations in the Iraq no-fly zones.

(3) In addition, RAF units are supporting UN Operations in the area of the former Yugoslavia - Operation Deny Flight, with transport units supplying essential items to areas such as Sarajevo, and fast jets operating from the airbase at Gioia de Colle in Italy to police the "no flying zone". In November 1993, Op Deny Flight involved the use of 8 x Tornado F3; 12 x Jaguar GR1; 2 x Sentry AEW 1 and 2 x Tristar.

Operational Conversion Units (OCU)

Tornado OCU (TWCU)	25 x Tornado GR1	RAF Lossiemouth	(15 Reserve Sqn)
Tornado F3 OCU	24 x Tornado F3	RAF Coningsby	(56 Reserve Sqn)
Jaguar OCU	10 x Jaguar	RAF Lossiemouth	(16 Reserve Sqn)
Harrier OCU	16 x Harrier	RAF Wittering	(20 Reserve Sqn)
Nimrod OCU	5 x Nimrod MR2P	RAF Kinloss	(42 Reserve Sqn)
Helicopter OCU	4 x Chinook; 5 x Puma	RAF Odiham	(27 Reserve Sqn)
Hercules OCU	5 x Hercules	RAF Lyneham	(57 Reserve Sqn)
VC-10/Tristar OCU	As required	RAF Brize Norton	(55 Reserve Sqn)

Royal Air Force Regiment

1 Sqn RAF Regt	RAF Laarbruch	Ground Defence
2 Sqn RAF Regt	RAF Catterick	Ground Defence (Honnington 1994)
3 Sqn RAF Regt	RAF Aldergrove	Ground Defence
15 Sqn RAF Regt	RAF Leeming	Rapier
19 Sqn RAF Regt	RAF Brize Norton	Rapier
20 Sqn RAF Regt	RAF Honnington	Rapier

26 Sqn RAF Regt	RAF Laarbruch	Rapier
27 Sqn RAF Regt	RAF Leuchars	Rapier
34 Sqn RAF Regt	RAF Akrotiri	Ground Defence/Light Armour
37 Sqn RAF Regt	RAF Bruggen	Rapier
48 Sqn RAF Regt	RAF Lossiemouth	Rapier
63 (QCS) Sqn	RAF Uxbridge	Ground Defence & Ceremonial
66 Sqn RAF Regt	RAF Honnington	Rapier
RAF Regt Depot	RAF Catterick	(Honington 1994)
Rapier Trg Unit	RAF West Raynham	(Honington 1994 - 16 Reserve Sqn)

Royal Auxiliary Air Force

No 1 Maritime HQ	Northwood (London)
No 2 Maritime HQ	Pitrivie (Scotland)
No 3 Maritime HQ	RAF St Mawgan
4624 Movements Sqn	RAF Brize Norton Air Movements
4626 Aeromedical Evacuation Sqn	RAF Hullavington

Royal Auxiliary Air Force Regiment

1310 Wing RAuxAF Regt	RAF Catterick	HQ Unit (Honnington 1994)
2503 Sqn RAuxAF Regt	RAF Waddington	Ground Defence
2620 Sqn RAuxAF Regt	RAF Marham	Ground Defence
2622 Sqn RAuxAF Regt	RAF Lossiemouth	Ground Defence
2624 Sqn RAuxAF Regt	RAF Brize Norton	Ground Defence
2625 Sqn RAuxAF Regt	RAF St Mawgan	Ground Defence
2729 Sqn RAuxAF Regt	RAF Waddington	Ground Defence
2890 Sqn RAuxAF Regt	RAF Waddington	Ground Defence

Royal Auxiliary Air Force Defence Force Flights

RAuxAF Defence Force Flight (Brampton)
RAuxAF Defence Force Flight (High Wycombe)
RAuxAF Defence Force Flight (Lyneham)
RAuxAF Defence Force Flight (St Athan)

Royal Air Force Volunteer Reserve

7000 Flight, Royal Air Force Volunteer Reserve
7010 Flight, Royal Air Force Volunteer Reserve
7630 Flight, Royal Air Force Volunteer Reserve
7644 Flight, Royal Air Force Volunteer Reserve

In war, these four flights would provide specialist assistance in public relations, foreign language interrogation, photographic interpretation and intelligence support.

Royal Air Force Volunteer Reserve - Airman Aircrew Augmentation

120 Sqn - Kinloss
201 Sqn - Kinloss

This programme covers a number of air electronics operators who fly Nimrod aircraft on maritime patrol.

Note: There are currently believed to be approximately 2,000 posts with the RAuxAF and a further 200 with the RAFVR. Proposals have been announced (1993) by the MOD for both of these organisations to be amalgamated.

Basic Flying Training

Elementary Flying Training Sqn	RAF Topcliffe	Civilian Aircraft
1 Flying Training School	RAF Linton-on-Ouse	Tucano
2 Flying Training School	RAF Shawbury	Gazelle/Wessex
3 Flying Training School	RAF Cranwell	Tucano

Advanced Flying Training

4 Flying Training School	RAF Valley	Hawk
6 Flying Training School	RAF Finningley	JP/Tucano/Hawk/Bulldog Jetstream/Dominie
7 Flying Training School	RAF Chivenor	Hawk (19 Reserve Sqn & (92 Reserve Sqn)
Central Flying School	RAF Scampton	Tucano/Bulldog/Hawk
Central Flying School	RAF Shawbury	Gazelle
Search & Rescue Training Unit	RAF Valley	Wessex
Sea King Training Unit	RAF St Mawga	Sea King

Miscellaneous Units

Queens Flight	3 x BAe 146, 2 x Wessex	RAF Benson
Red Arrows	11 x Hawk	RAF Scampton
TTTE	17 x Tornado GR1	RAF Cottesmore*

Note*: TTTU - Trinational Tornado Training Unit. The 17 x Tornado GR1 are British aircraft. There are also German and Italian aircraft present.

British Airline Fleets

In an emergency, the Government has the power to enlist the assistance of the United Kingdoms civil airline fleets. In total there appear to be 34 registered airlines operating approximately 650 x fixed wing, passenger and transport aircraft.

The largest of these airlines is British Airways with some 50,000 employees operating 241 aircraft, and during 1992/93 British Airways carried over 28 million passengers and 500,000 tons of freight. Other major British airlines include Air UK with 28 aircraft. Britannia Airways the world's largest charter airline with 33 aircraft, and who carried nearly 7 million passengers in 1992. British Midland Airways with 31 aircraft and Virgin Atlantic with 16 aircraft.

The composition of British Airway's fleet as at 31 March 1993 was as follows:

Aircraft	Owned	Leased	Total	Future Deliveries	Options
Concorde	7		7		
Boeing 747-100	15		15		
Boeing 747-200	13	3	16		
Boeing 747-400	12	13	25	36	22
Boeing 777				15	15
Tristar 1 and 100	5		5		
MD DC-10-30	5	2	7		
Boeing 767-300	9	11	20	8	9
Boeing 757-200	37	5	42	3	1
Airbus 320	10		10		
Boeing 737-200	23	16	39		
Boeing 737-300		3	3		
Boeing 737-400	18	14	32	6	10
BAC 1-11-500	6		6		
BAe ATP		14	14		6
Totals	**160**	**81**	**241**	**68**	**63**

THE DEFENCE BUDGET

*"You need three things to win a war,
Money, money and more money"*

Trivulzio (1441-1518)

The UK Government plans to spend the following amounts on defence during the period 1993-1997:

1993-94 -£23.41 billion
1994-95 -£23.49 billion
1995-96 -£22.70 billion
1996-97 -£22.79 billion

Overall Defence Expenditure is expected to fall by 12% in real terms between 1990-91 and 1995-96, with defence spending representing approximately 3.9% of GDP (Gross Domestic Product) in 1992-93, and declining to about 3.2% of GDP in 1995-96. In 1985 defence expenditure represented 5.2% of GDP.

The total Central Government Expenditure during the FY 1994-95 is budgeted at £251.3 million, and for comparison the government's major expenditure programmes during FY 1994-95 are as follows:

Defence	£23.4 billion
Overseas Aid	£2.3 billion
Health	£31.7 billion
Transport	£5.8 billion
Housing	£7.4 billion
Home Office	£6.2 billion
Education	£10.4 billion
Social Security	£68.8 billion
Agriculture	£2.8 billion
Foreign Office	£1.2 billion
Employment	£3.7 billion
Local Government	£29.9 billion
Scotland	£14.1 billion
Wales	£6.6 billion
Northern Ireland	£7.3 billion

The breakdown of the 1993-94 Defence Budget figure of £23.41 billion pounds can be shown in percentage terms for all three services as follows:

Equipment Purchases	- 39%
Service Personnel	- 29%
Civilian Personnel	- 13%
Works and Miscellaneous Services	- 19%

The equipment expenditure figure at 39% of the total can be broken down further, to reveal that during the 1993-94 Financial Year a total of £9.9 billion pounds will be spent, with money going to the services as follows:

Naval Equipment	-£2.59 billion
Army Equipment	-£1.87 billion
Air Equipment	-£3.21 billion
General Support	-£2.22 billion

(These figures include expenditure on research, development, production and repair).

RAF Expenditure

Some of the more interesting Air Force expenditure figures for the 1993-94 Financial Year are amongst the following:

RAF Strike Command

	£ Million
Offensive, reconnaissance and transport aircraft	676.0
Air Defence of the UK	382.5
Maritime aircraft and SAR	265.7
RAF Germany	268.5
Admin support and financial management	179.1
	1771.8

Air Member for Personnel

RAF Personnel Management	77.6
Personnel support	8.1
Trainees	111.6
	197.3

RAF Support Command

Training	351.7
Maintenance, logistics and signals support	371.6
Administrative Support	129.8
	853.1

Air Member for Supply & Organisation

Material management and movements planning	1,184.1
Support services including communications electronics and logistical information technology	210.2
National Air Traffic Service	43.1
	1437.4

Procurement Executive

Controller Air	45.2
Controller Air (Nuclear)	652.1
	697.3

The high unit costs of individual items of equipment illustrate the problems faced by defence planners when working out their annual budgets. At 1994 prices the following items cost:

Tornado GR1	£20 million
Tornado F3	£30 million
Harrier GR5/7	£15 million
Lynx Helicopter	£6 million
New Army Attack Helicopter	£14 million
Rapier Missile	£35,000

Air Charter Costs

The total sums allocated to air charter in the MOD supply budgets for the years 1990-93 were as follows:

1990 - 1991	£13.41 million
1991 - 1992	£13.21 million
1992 - 1993	£16.09 million

Running Costs

The average running costs for some RAF organisations during 1992-93 were as follows:

Nimrod MR Sqn	£18.8 million
Jaguar GR1a Sqn	£19.4 million
Buccaneer Sqn	£19.7 million
Tornado GR1 Sqn	£26.7 million
Tornado F3 Sqn	£35.6 million
Annual cost of Red Arrows (1992-93)	£17 million
Annual cost of RAF C-130 fleet (1992-93)	£140 million

During 1990-91 the Royal Air Force spent £78.4 million on fuel for heating and lighting.

DEFENCE SPENDING - NATO COMPARISON

The nations of the North Atlantic Treaty Organisation (NATO), of which the United Kingdom is a member state, spent some US$ 419.9 billion (£279.9 billion) on defence during FY 1993 (the latest year for which all of the relevant data is available). The following table shows the actual 1993 defence expenditure by each NATO nation.

USA	US$ 258.6bn
France	US$ 35.8 bn

UK	US$ 35.2 bn
Germany	US$ 31.2 bn
Italy	US$ 16.5 bn
Canada	US$ 9.6 bn
Spain	US$ 6.5 bn
Netherlands	US$ 7.3 bn
Turkey	US$ 5.0 bn
Greece	US$ 4.4 bn
Norway	US$ 3.2 bn
Belgium	US$ 2.9 bn
Denmark	US$ 2.2 bn
Portugal	US$ 1.5 bn
Luxembourg	US$ 98.9 million

Note: Iceland has no military expenditure although it remains a member of NATO. An interesting comparison is made by the total national defence budget divided by the total number of full time personnel in all three services. Figures for the top five world defence spending nations are as follows:

Nation	1993 Defence Budget	1993 Total Service Personnel	Cost Per Serviceman
USA	US$258.6 bn	1,729,700	US$149,505
UK	US$35.2 bn	274,800	US$132,082
France	US$35.8 bn	411,600	US$86,977
Japan	US$39.7 bn	237,700	US$167,017
Germany	US$31.2 bn	408,200	US$76,433

Note: Russia should feature in this table but, because of hyper-inflation, it is currently impossible to make a meaningful conversion from Roubles to US$. In addition, our latest research suggests that the Russian Government is not entirely certain regarding its manpower figures and expenditure totals.

ROYAL AIR FORCE STATISTICS (as at 1 February 1994)

	1994	1980
Strike/Attack Squadrons	6	14
Offensive Support Squadrons	5	5
Air Defence Squadrons	6	16
Maritime Patrol Squadrons	3	4
Reconnaissance Squadrons	5	5
Airborne Early Warning Squadrons	1	1
Transport Squadrons	13	9
Tanker Squadrons	1	2

Search & Rescue Squadrons	2	2
Surface to Air Missile Squadrons	5	8
Ground Defence Squadrons	4	5
	51	**71**

Note: 1980 Figures are for comparison purposes.

Royal Air Force Personnel Strengths (As at 1 April 1993)

Males	1980	1993
Officers	14.1	13.3 In Thousands
Servicemen	69.4	60.7

Females		
Officers	0.7	1.1
Servicewomen	5.4	5.7
Total	**89.6**	**80.9**

Note: Current plans envisage a total RAF strength of 72,100 by 1 April 1994 following extensive redundancies.

Deployment of The Royal Air Force (As at 1 April 1993)

Support Command	Uniformed UK Based Personnel	Civilians
Training	7,800	2,800
Maint, Logistics and Signals	7,700	6,200
Admin Support	3,100	1,200
Total	**18,600**	**10,200**

Strike Command

Offensive, Reconnaissance & Transport Aircraft	19,700	1,900
UK Air Defence	11,300	1,200
Maritime Aircraft & SAR	7,500	1,000
RAF Germany	7,000	100
Admin & Financial Support	3,300	600
Total	**48,800**	**4,800**

Air Member for Personnel

RAF Personnel Management	1,600	700
Personnel Support	800	200

Trainees & Non Effective Staff	3,100	Nil
Total	**5,500**	**900**

Air Member for Supply & Organisation

Material Management	700	1,500
Supply Services	1,000	200
Total	**1,700**	**1,700**

Chief of Defence Procurement

Controller Air	100	1,200
Controller Air (Nuclear)	Nil	300
Total	**100**	**1,500**

Note: All totals are rounded to the nearest thousand.

Deployment of the Royal Air Force - Geographical (at 1 April 1993)

United Kingdom	68,129
RAF Germany	7,000
Gibraltar	336
Cyprus	1,621
Elsewhere in Continental Europe	1,022
Mediterranean, Near East & the Gulf	390
Hong Kong	256
Elsewhere in the Far East	19
	2,127

Other Locations

Note: The figures for UK and Europe include personnel who are posted on detachment to other areas such as Cyprus, Belize, Falkland Islands, Canada and the Gulf.

Deployment of the Royal Air Force - Operational Squadrons

During mid 1993 the following numbers of RAF personnel were engaged on duties with operational squadrons as follows:

Tornado GR1 Sqns	1,455
Tornado F3 Sqns	930
Nimrod R & MR	551
Jaguar	446

Harrier	416
Canberra PR9	103
Airborne Early Warning	165
Transport, Tanker & SAR	2,630

Figures relate to squadron personnel for each aircraft fleet but do not include OCUs/TWCU personnel. Therefore the average Tornado F3 Sqn has 133 personnel and the average Tornado GR1 Sqn 180.

Royal Air Force - Reserves

Regular Reserves

	1993	1980
Males	44,300	29,800
Females	1,800	500
Total	**46,100**	**30,300**

Volunteer Reserves and Auxiliary Forces

Males	1,400	400
Females	300	100
Total	**1,700**	**500**

Royal Air Force - Uniformed Medical Personnel (At 1 Apr 1993)

Doctors	368
Dentists	119
Nurses	2,038 (Figure includes males, females and support staff).

Royal Air Force - Recruitment (During Financial Year 1992/93)

	(1992-93)	(1990/91)	(1980/81)
Male Officers	247	614	885
Servicemen	643	4,508	8,763
Female Officers	70	169	158
Servicewomen	198	1,506	1,049
Total	**1,158**	**6,797**	**10,855**

Note: Previous years figures are given for comparison.

Outflow - Royal Air Force (During Financial Year 1992/93)

	(1992-93)	(1990/91)	(1980/81)
Male Officers	857	918	659
Servicemen	4,633	6,088	5,242
Female Officers	134	135	98
Servicewomen	592		1,005
929			
Total	**6,216**	**8,147**	**6,928**

RAF Engagement Extension Requests

During 1992-1993 the following numbers of RAF personnel applied to extend their service:

Officers	339
Servicemen/women	4,262
Total	**4,601**

Royal Air Force Cadets

	(1 Apr 1993)	(1 Jan 1980)
Males	34,100	43,900
Females	9,900	200
Total	**44,000**	**44,100**

Note: Includes members of the Combined Cadet Force and the Air Training Corps, but excludes officers, training and administrative staff.

Officer to Other Ranks Ratio

For comparison purposes, the ratio of officers to other ranks in each of the three UK Armed Services in 1980 and 1992 was:

	1992	1980
Royal Air Force	1:4.7	1:5.1
Army	1:7.4	1:8.3
Royal Navy & Royal Marines	1:5.2	1:6.1
All Services	1:5.9	1:6.6

Ministry of Defence - Civilian Employment

At September 1st 1993, the UK MOD employed 128,000 civil servants of whom 41,000 were employed in industrial grades, 54,000 were specialist non-industrials and 33,000 were administrative. In the Whitehall area, some 3,400 full-time and part-time civil servants are employed and rents in this area are expected to be in the region of £58 million during the FY year 1993-94. Of this figure of £58 million, about £30million will go to the Department of the Environment.

On the 1st January 1988, MOD civilian employment was 144,800. This means that civilian employment has fallen by 11.6% during the period that uniformed strength has fallen by 15.8%.

RAF Station Manning - Illustrative Example

Before closure, and during 1991 whilst still operating 2 x Phantom and 1 x Pembroke Squadron, personnel totals at RAF Wildenrath were as follows:

	Total	
Officers		
Operations	113	
Engineering	20	
Administration	33	
Medical/Dental	7	
	Total 173	
Airmen/Airwomen		
Aircraft Engineering	466	
Ground Engineering	229	
Operations	63	
Supply	144	
Administration	312	
Medical	14	
Dental	5	
	Total 1,233	Station Total 1,406

CHAPTER 2 - ORGANISATIONS

"Every time you reorganise - you bleed" - Pentagon Folk Wisdom

In late 1963, the three independent service ministries, the War Office (Army), Air Ministry (Royal Air Force) and the Admiralty (Royal Navy) were merged to form the unified United Kingdom Ministry of Defence (MOD). This large organisation, that directly affects the lives of over three quarters of a million servicemen, reservists and MOD civilians, is controlled by the Secretary of State for Defence, who is also the chairman of the Defence Council.

The Defence Council is the organisation that makes the policy decisions to ensure the three fighting services are run efficiently, and in accordance with the wishes of the government of the day. The composition of the Defence Council is as follows:

Defence Council
The Secretary of State for Defence

Minister of State (Armed Forces)	Chief of the Defence Staff
Minister of State (Defence Procurement)	Vice-Chief of the Defence Staff
Permanant Under Secretary of State	Chief of the Naval Staff
Chief Scientific Adviser	Chief of the Air Staff
Chief of Personnel & Logistics	Chief of the General Staff
Chief of the Procurement Executive	

The routine management of the Royal Air Force is the Responsibility of the Air Force Board, the composition of which is shown in the next diagram:

Air Force Board
The Secretary of State for Defence

Minister of State (Armed Forces)	Chief of the Air Staff
Minister of State (Defence Procurement)	Air Member for Personnel
Under Secretary of State (Armed Forces)	Controller of Aircraft
Under Secretary of State Air (Defence Procurement)	Member for Logistics
	AOC Strike Command
2nd Permanant Under Secretary of State	Assistant Chief of Air Staff

Decisions made by the Defence Council or the Air Force Board are implemented by the air staff at various headquarters world-wide. The Chief of the Air Staff is the officer ultimately responsible for the Royal Air Force's contribution to the national defence effort. He maintains control through the AOC (Air Officer Commanding), and the staff branches of each of these headquarters. Operational Headquarters are now organised as under the NATO system with the following designations for the staff branches:

Staff Branches

The Staff Branches that you would expect to find at every level in a headquarters from the Ministry of Defence down to station level are as follows:

Commander -   Usually known as the AOC (Air Officer Commanding).

Chief of Staff -   The officer who runs the headquarters on a day-to-day basis and who often acts as a second-in-command.

G1 Branch -   Responsible for personnel matters including manning, discipline and personal services.

G2 Branch -   Responsible for intelligence and security

G3 Branch -   Responsible for operations including staff duties, exercise planning, training, operational requirements, combat development & tactical doctrine.

G4 Branch -   Logistics and quartering.

G5 Branch -   Civil and military co-operation.

An operational headquarters in the field will almost certainly be a tri-service organisation with branches from the Army, Navy and Air Force represented. The Staff Branches are the same for all three services.

Royal Air Force - Chain of Command (Pre 1 April 1994)

The Royal Air Force is controlled from the MOD via two major headquarters and a number of smaller headquarters world-wide. The following diagram illustrates this chain-of-command.

Chief of the Air Staff
Commander - Air Chief Marshal
(Ministry of Defence)

RAF Strike Command Commander - Air Chief Marshal (High Wycombe)	RAF Support Command Commander - Air Marshal (Brampton)

Chain of Command - Post 1 April 1994

On the 1st April 1994, Support Command will be divided into two command and administrative groups and the chain of command will be as follows:

Chief of the Air Staff
Commander - Air Chief Marshal
(Ministry of Defence)

HQSTC RAF Strike Command Air Chief Marshal (High Wycombe)	HQPTC RAF Personnel & Training Air Chief Marshal Command (Innsworth)	HQLC RAF Logistics Command Air Chief Marshal (Brampton)

Strike Command

Following April 1994 changes to the RAF Chain of Command, it is believed that the essential framework of Strike Command will remain as it is at present (January 1994) based around 5 major groups. The composition of these Strike Command Groups is shown in detail in the Commands Chapter. In general these 5 Groups are responsible for:

1 Group	- Strike/Attack
2 Group	- Germany/ARRC Support
11 Group	- Air Defence
18 Group	- Maritime Patrol and SAR
38 Group	- Air Transport and Communications

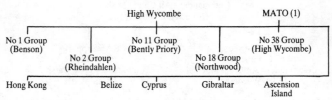

HQ Strike Command

High Wycombe — MATO (1)

No 1 Group (Benson)	No 2 Group (Rheindahlen)	No 11 Group (Bently Priory)	No 18 Group (Northwood)	No 38 Group (High Wycombe)
Hong Kong	Belize	Cyprus	Gibraltar	Ascension Island

(1) Military Air Traffic Organisation.

In addition to these major units, Strike Command has the following organisations included in its order of battle.

Tornado Operational Evaluation Unit
Strike Attack Operational Evaluation Unit
Institute of Aviation Medicine

Personnel & Training Command

The following is a guide to the outline of the new RAF PTC, more detail is included in the next chapter.

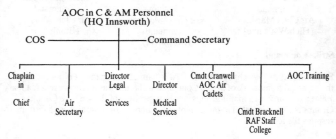

AOC in C & AM Personnel
(HQ Innsworth)

COS —————— Command Secretary

| Chaplain in Chief | Air Secretary | Director Legal Services | Director Medical Services | Cmdt Cranwell AOC Air Cadets | Cmdt Bracknell RAF Staff College | AOC Training |

Logistic Command (LC)

The following is a guide to the outline of the new RAF LC, more detail is included in the next chapter.

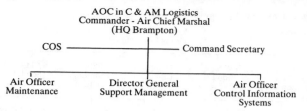

AOC in C & AM Logistics
Commander - Air Chief Marshal
(HQ Brampton)

COS ——————————— Command Secretary

Air Officer
Maintenance

Director General
Support Management

Air Officer
Control Information
Systems

RAF Station Organisation

An indication of the manner in which an RAF Station might be organised is as
follows. Our example is an RAF Station with 3 x Tornado GR1 flying squadrons -
each with 12 x aircraft. The 36 aircraft will have cost at least 720 million pounds in
total purchase costs, and the combined running costs for the operation of these
three squadrons will be in the region of some 80 million pounds per annum.

Station Commander
(Group Captain)

Tornado GR1   Tornado GR1   Tornado GR1
Sqn   Sqn   Sqn

Operations(1)   Administration(2)   Engineering(3)
Wing   Wing   Wing

Notes: (1) Ops Wing; (2) Admin Wing; (3) Eng Wing; (4) Expect
the commanders of the Tornado Sqns to be Wing Commanders
aged between 34-40. Ops, Admin and Eng Wings will almost
certainly be commanded by Wing Commanders from their
respective branch specialities - these Wing Commanders will
probably be a little older than the commanders of the flying
squadrons.

Flying Squadron Organisation

Sqn Commander
(Wing Commander)

Flight Commander   Flight Commander   Department
(Sqn Leader)   (Sqn Leader)   Leaders(1)
6 x Tornado GR1   6 x Tornado GR1

Note: (1) These departmental leaders have responsibility for weapons, airframes,
propulsion, electronics, flight guidance and control systems, communications,
automatic navigation and attack controls and report to the squadron commander.

Operations Wing Organisation

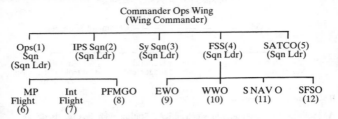

Notes: (1) Operations Sqn; (2) Intelligence & Planning Sqn; (3) Security Sqn - includes RAF Police & Station Defence Personnel; (4) Flying Support Sqn; (5) Senior Air Traffic Control Officer; (6) Mission Plans Flight; (7) Intelligence Flight; (8) Pre-flight Message Generation Officer; (9) Electronic Warfare Officer; (10) Wing Weapon Officer; (11) Senior Navigation Officer; (12) Station Safety Officer.

Administration Wing Organisation

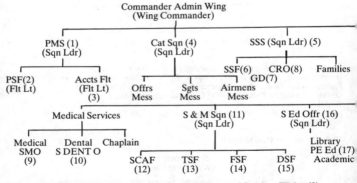

Notes: (1) Personnel Management Squadron; (2) Personal Services Flight; (3) Accounts Flight; (4) Catering Sqn; (5) Station Services Sqn; (6) Station Services Flight; (7) General Duties Flight; (8) Community Relations Officer (9) Senior Medical Officer; (10) Senior Dental Officer; (11) Supply & Movements Sqn; (12) Supply Control & Accounts Flight; (13) Technical Supply Flight; (14) Forward Supply Flight; (15) Domestic Supply Flight; (16) Senior Education Officer; (17) Phyisicial Education.

Engineering Wing (Diagram Overleaf)

Notes: (1) Engineering Ops; (2) Mechanical Engineering Aircraft Sqn; (3) Aircraft Servicing Flight; (4) Aircraft Components Flight; (5) Propulsion Flight; (6)

Mechanical Engineering Ground Squadron; (7) Mechanical Transport; (8) General Engineering Flight; (9) Armament Engineering Sqn; (10) Armament Engineering Flight; (11) Weapon Storage Flight; (12) (13) Electrical Engineering Squadron; (14) Ground Radio Servicing Fliight; (15) Avionics Electrical Systems Flight; (16) Tornado Navigation Systems Flight; (17) Navigation and Attack Systems Flight.

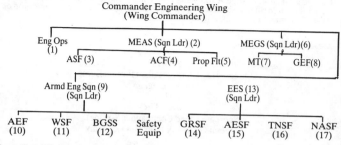

Operational Conversion Unit (OCU)

The RAF has a number of OCU's designed to train pilots for front line squadron service as follows:

Tornado OCU (TWCU)	25 x Tornado GR1	RAF Lossiemouth	(15 Reserve Sqn)
Tornado F3 OCU	24 x Tornado F3	RAF Coningsby	(56 Reserve Sqn)
Jaguar OCU	10 x Jaguar	RAF Lossiemouth	(16 Reserve Sqn)
Harrier OCU	16 x Harrier	RAF Wittering	(20 Reserve Sqn)
Nimrod OCU	5 x Nimrod MR2	RAF Kinloss	(42 Reserve Sqn)
Helicopter OCU	4 x Chinook; 5 x Puma	RAF Odiham	(27 Reserve Sqn)
Hercules OCU	5 x Hercules	RAF Lyneham	(57 Reserve Sqn)
VC-10/Tristar	As required	RAFBrize Norton	(55 Reserve Sqn)

The organisation of an OCU is obviously tailored to fit the size of the aircraft fleet being supported. As an example No 56 Reserve Sqn (Tornado F3 OCU) is organised along the following lines:

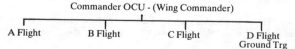

A and B Flights provide flying training with about 23 x staff crews and 12 x student crews. C Flight is a standards flight - training instructors, and D Flight provides simulators and a dome air combat trainer.

NATO COMMAND STRUCTURE

Following re-organisations taking effect from 1 July 1993, NATO was reorganised from three into two major Commands. The first is ACLANT (Allied Command

Atlantic with headquarters at Norfolk, Virginia (USA) and the second is ACE (Allied Command Europe), with its headquarters at Mons in Belgium.

Operations in the European area in which the United Kingdom was a participant would almost certainly be as part of a NATO force under the command and control of Allied Command Europe (ACE). The current Supreme Allied Commander Europe is General George A Joulwan of the United States Army who replaced General John M Shalikashvili on the 4th of October 1993. The new organisation of Allied Command Europe is as follows:

Allied Command Europe

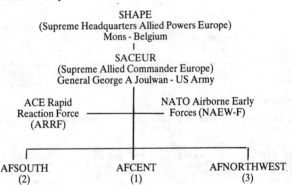

Notes:

(1) AFCENT - Allied Forces Central European Theatre with headquarters at Brunssum in the Netherlands and with overall responsibility for military operations in Central Europe. AFCENT is further subdivided into three subordinate commands - see next diagram.

(2) AFSOUTH - Allied Forces Southern Europe, with headquarters at Naples in Italy and responsible for military operations in the area of Turkey, Greece and Italy.

(3) AFNORTHWEST - Allied Forces North-western Europe, with headquarters at High Wycombe in the UK. This new headquarters, that will be operational as from 1 July 1994 and will be responsible for operations in Norway, the UK, and the maritime area between the two countries. The Chief of Staff (Designate) is Lieutenant General Ola Aabakken of the Norwegian Army.

HQ AFNORTHWEST will be leaner and more efficient than its predecessor AFNORTH at Oslo in Norway, and will be ready for operations in July 1994. The headquarters will be staffed by about 300 personnel, the first of whom will begin to arrive at High Wycombe with their families in March of 1994. The majority of the headquarters staff will be British, American and Norwegian, but Belgium, Canada, Denmark, Germany and the Netherlands will be represented.

Following re-organisation the composition of AFCENT is as follows:

Allied Forces Central European Theatre

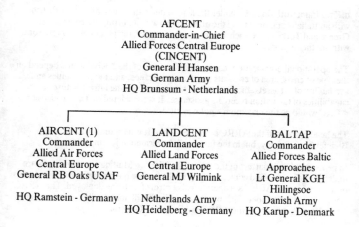

AFCENT
Commander-in-Chief
Allied Forces Central Europe
(CINCENT)
General H Hansen
German Army
HQ Brunssum - Netherlands

AIRCENT (1)
Commander
Allied Air Forces
Central Europe
General RB Oaks USAF

HQ Ramstein - Germany

LANDCENT
Commander
Allied Land Forces
Central Europe
General MJ Wilmink

Netherlands Army
HQ Heidelberg - Germany

BALTAP
Commander
Allied Forces Baltic
Approaches
Lt General KGH
Hillingsoe
Danish Army
HQ Karup - Denmark

Note:

(1) AIRCENT is now responsible for all air forces in the AFCENT region.
(2) The AFCENT operational area now includes Northern Germany and Denmark, extending 800 kms to the south to the Swiss and Austrian borders.

The Allied Rapid Reaction Corps (ARRC)

Air operations on the European mainland will most probably be in support of the ARRC. This formation is the land component of the Allied Command Europe Rapid Reaction Forces and it will be prepared for employment in support of SACEUR'S crisis management options whenever necessary. Its peacetime planning structure includes 10 divisions plus corps troops from from 12 NATO nations to allow a rapid response to a wide range of eventualities.

The ARRC will consist of :

a. National divisions from Germany, the United Kingdom and the United States; Spain will also provide a division under special co-ordination agreements.

b. The Multinational Division (MND-C), which will include Belgian, German, Dutch and British airmobile units.

c. The Multinational Division (MND-S), which will include Greek, Italian and Turkish units.

d. Two framework divisions under the lead of one nation: one of these is British with an Italian component and the other Italian with a Portuguese component. Greece and Turkey have each assigned a division with the potential to framework with another nation.

The operational organisation, composition and size of the ARRC would depend on the type of crisis, area of crisis, its political significance, and the capabilities and availability of lift assets, the distances to be covered and the infrastructure capabilities of the nation receiving assistance. It is considered that a four-division ARRC would be the maximum employment structure.

The headquarters of the ARRC is multinational. It is temporarily located at Bielefeld in Germany, but in the future will be located in Rheindahlen.

In peace, the headquarters of the ARRC and the two Multinational Divisions are under the command and control of SACEUR, but the remaining divisions and units only come under SACEUR's operational control after being deployed. The ARRC was activated in October 1992, but the corps itself will not be fully operational until 1995. The commander of the ARRC is a British Lt General.

The main British contribution to the ARRC is 1 (UK) Armoured Division that is stationed in Germany and has a considerable number of British personnel in both the ARRC Corps HQ and Corps Troops. In addition, in times of tension 3(UK) Div and 24 Airmobile Bde will move to the European mainland to take their place in the ARRC's order of battle. In total, we believe that some 55,000 British Regular soldiers could be assigned to the ARRC (23,000 resident in Germany) together with substantial numbers of Regular Army Reservists and formed TA Units.

The mission statement of the ARRC is as follows:

"Be prepared to deploy ARRC forces of corps troops and up to four divisions on military operations in support of SACEUR's crisis management options".

Outline Composition of the ARRC (ACE Rapid Reaction Corps)

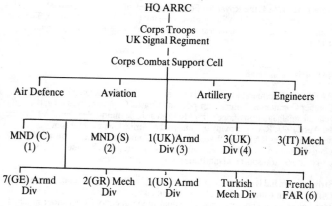

Notes: (1) MND(C) - Multinational Division - Central; (2) Multinational Division - South (3) Resident in Germany (4) Resident in the UK the structure of 3(UK) Division is outlined in the Miscellaneous Chapter.
(5) IT - Italy; GE - Germany; GR - Greece;(6) FAR - Rapid Action Force.

CHAPTER 3 - RAF COMMANDS

From 1 April 1994, the Royal Air Force is divided into three operational Commands. These are RAF Logistic Command (LC), RAF Personnel & Training Command (PTC), and the largest and most important, RAF Strike Command (STC).

RAF Strike Command

RAF Strike Command was formed on April 30, 1968, by merging Fighter and Bomber Commands. Later, Transport and Coastal Commands joined in the general amalgamation of operations to form a single multi-role Command. On the 1st April 1993, RAF Germany became part of Strike Command. From its headquarters at RAF High Wycombe, Strike Command now controls all of the United Kingdom's front-line aircraft world-wide. Its assets include fighters, strike/attack, transport and maritime aircraft and helicopters.

Strike Command is also an essential part of the NATO organisation. As the Air Officer Commanding-in-Chief Strike Command (AOCinC STC), Air Chief Marshal Sir John Thompson holds the dual appointment of Commander-in-Chief United Kingdom Air Forces (CINCUKAIR) - a NATO appointment.

As the commander of Strike Command the AOCinC is responsible for the day to day national peacetime operations of the Command. As CINCUKAIR he is also responsible to the Supreme Allied Commander Europe (SACEUR) for the defence of the UK Air Defence Region (UKADR) and the provision of combat-ready air forces to support other NATO commands.

HQSTC at High Wycombe is also a four star headquarters for out-of-theatre operations, and was Joint Headquarters (JHQ) for Operation Granby (to liberate Kuwait) and Operation Haven (to provide assistance to Kurdish refugees on the Turkish/Iraqi border). HQSTC is currently (March 1994) the JHQ for Op Warden and Op Jural (to moniter and deter air activity over Northern and Southern Iraq respectively), Op Cheshire (to fly supplies to the former Yugoslavia), and Op Deny Flight (to enforce the No-Fly Zone over Bosnia).

As of March 1993, the Command controls about 5,000 civilians and 45,000 servicemen and women - over half of the present strength of the Royal Air Force and operates some 800 aircraft. The personnel and aircraft are spread through some 200 units of various sizes, the majority of which are in the United Kindom. Strike Command is based upon five core groups:**Strike Command Organisation**

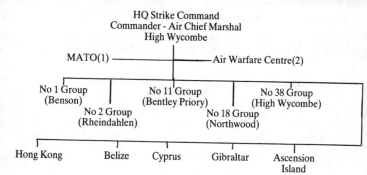

HQ Strike Command
Commander - Air Chief Marshal
High Wycombe

MATO(1) ———————— Air Warfare Centre(2)

No 1 Group (Benson)
No 2 Group (Rheindahlen)
No 11 Group (Bentley Priory)
No 18 Group (Northwood)
No 38 Group (High Wycombe)

Hong Kong | Belize | Cyprus | Gibraltar | Ascension Island

Notes:
(1) MATO stands for Military Air Traffic Organisation.
(2) The Air Warfare Centre (formerly CTTO) is responsible for the Tornado F3 OEU and the SAOEU.
(3) Cyprus has Group Status within Strike Command.
(4) Groups are normally commanded by Air Vice Marshals although the commander of 18 Group is an Air Marshal.

In general these 5 Groups are responsible for:

1 Group	-	Strike/Attack/Army Support
2 Group	-	Germany/ARRC Support
11 Group	-	Air Defence
18 Group	-	Maritime Patrol EW and SAR
38 Group	-	Air Transport, Communications & AAR

No 1 Group

HQ No 1 Group
RAF Benson - Strike/Attack/Army Support

Harrier	Tornado	Jaguar	Chinook	Puma/Wessex
1 Sqn	2 Sqn GR1A	6 Sqn	7 Sqn	33 Sqn
20 Sqn(R)	13 Sqn GRIA	16 Sqn(R)		60 Sqn
	15 Sqn(R) GR1	41 Sqn		72 Sqn
	TTTE	54 Sqn		230 Sqn
				27 Sqn(R)

No 1 Group has the following RAF Regiment Squadrons under command:

| No 2 Sqn RAF Regt | - | Honnington | - | Field Squadron |
| No 3 Sqn RAF Regt | - | Aldergrove | - | Field Squadron |

Flying Stations

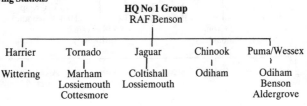

HQ No 1 Group
RAF Benson

Harrier	Tornado	Jaguar	Chinook	Puma/Wessex
Wittering	Marham	Coltishall	Odiham	Odiham
	Lossiemouth	Lossiemouth		Benson
	Cottesmore			Aldergrove

No 2 Group

HQ No 2 Group
Rheindahlen - Germany/ARRC Support

Harrier	Tornado	Puma/Chinook	Berlin Station
3 Sqn	9 Sqn GR1	18 Sqn	Flight
4 Sqn	14 Sqn GR1		2 x Chipmunk *
	17 Sqn GR1		
	31 Sqn GR1	* Closure Shortly	

Low level air defence of airfields is provided by Rapier equipped Air Defence squadrons of the RAF Regiment. No 2 Group has the following RAF Regiment Squadrons under command:

No 1 Sqn RAF Regt	-	Laarbruch	-	Field Squadron
No 26 Sqn RAF Regt	-	Laarbruch	-	Rapier
No 37 Sqn RAF Regt	-	Bruggen	-	Rapier

No 2 Group also has the following under command:

RAF Decimomannu (Sardinia)	-	Air Combat & Weapons Training
RAF Nordhorn	-	Air Weapons Training Facility
RAF (Hospital)	-	Wegberg
RAF Signals Unit	-	Bruggen
RAF Signals Unit	-	Rheindahlen

Flying Stations

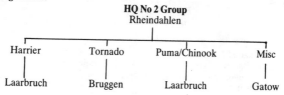

HQ No 2 Group
Rheindahlen

Harrier	Tornado	Puma/Chinook	Misc
Laarbruch	Bruggen	Laarbruch	Gatow

No 11 Group

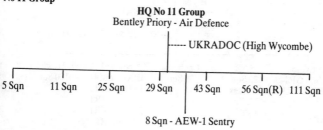

HQ No 11 Group
Bentley Priory - Air Defence

------ UKRADOC (High Wycombe)

5 Sqn   11 Sqn   25 Sqn   29 Sqn   43 Sqn   56 Sqn(R)   111 Sqn

8 Sqn - AEW-1 Sentry

Note: All of these Sqns are equipped with Tornado F3.

Low level air defence of airfields is provided by Rapier equipped Air Defence
squadrons of the RAF Regiment. No 11 Group has the following RAF Regiment
Squadrons under command:

No 15 Sqn RAF Regt	-	Leeming	-	Rapier
No 27 Sqn RAF Regt	-	Leuchars	-	Rapier
No 48 Sqn RAF Regt	-	Lossiemouth	-	Rapier

Also included under command No 11 Group are:

Tornado F3 OEU	-	Coningsby
Sentry Training Squadron	-	Waddington
Battle of Britian Memorial Flight	-	Coningsby

Flying Stations

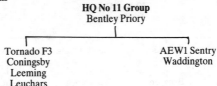

HQ No 11 Group
Bentley Priory

Tornado F3
Coningsby
Leeming
Leuchars

AEW1 Sentry
Waddington

No 18 Group

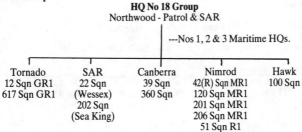

HQ No 18 Group
Northwood - Patrol & SAR

---Nos 1, 2 & 3 Maritime HQs.

Tornado	SAR	Canberra	Nimrod	Hawk
12 Sqn GR1	22 Sqn	39 Sqn	42(R) Sqn MR1	100 Sqn
617 Sqn GR1	(Wessex)	360 Sqn	120 Sqn MR1	
	202 Sqn		201 Sqn MR1	
	(Sea King)		206 Sqn MR1	
			51 Sqn R1	

Flying Stations

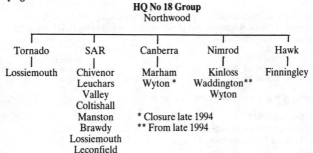

HQ No 18 Group
Northwood

Tornado	SAR	Canberra	Nimrod	Hawk
Lossiemouth	Chivenor	Marham	Kinloss	Finningley
	Leuchars	Wyton *	Waddington**	
	Valley		Wyton	
	Coltishall			
	Manston	* Closure late 1994		
	Brawdy	** From late 1994		
	Lossiemouth			
	Leconfield			

36

No 18 Group has the following units under command:

SARTU (Search & Rescue Training Unit)	-	Valley
SKTU (Sea King Training Unit)	-	St Mawgan

The main activities of No 18 Group are maritime surface and subsurface surveillance, search and rescue (SAR) and regular patrolling of the North Sea oil and gas installations, and fishery limits. Tasks are controlled from the Air Headquarters at Northwood, Middlesex. In war, the Nimrods would operate under the Supreme Allied Commander Atlantic (SACLANT), the AOC No 18 Group holding the NATO post of Commander Maritime Air Eastern Atlantic (COMMAIREASTLANT). As such, his main tasks would be to provide maritime strike/attack, maritime reconnaissance and anti-submarine support for naval operations and in protection of allied merchant shipping.

The major headquarters for co-ordinating this activity are:

No 1 Maritime HQ	-	Northwood
No 2 Maritime HQ	-	Pitrivie
No 3 Maritime HQ	-	St Mawgan

The UK MOD recently announced the opening of a Joint Maritime Communications Centre (JMCC) at St Mawgan in Cornwall. When the headquarters is operational in 1996, some 400 personnel will be associated with the JMCC of whom about 50% will be US Navy. Of about 200 UK personnel, 50% will be from the Royal Navy and 50% from the RAF. The UK MOD will pay for the JMCC building and the US will pay for the equipment. The JMCC comprises a buried, hardened communications building approximately 70 metres square within the perimeter of RAF St Mawgan. The centre will be integrated within the existing RAF fixed communications system, and will include two additional satellite ground terminals, each approximately 3 metres in diameter, also sited within the station boundary.

No 18 Group controls SAR through the Rescue Co-ordination Centres at Plymouth and Edinburgh. The Group's search and rescue Sea King and Wessex helicopters with, where appropriate, the Nimrods and marine craft units, are frequently engaged in rescue work and mercy flights, saving several hundred lives each year. The Group is also responsible for photographic reconnaissance cover using Canberra PR9. The Canberra PR unit also undertakes photographic surveys for the Ministry of Defence and other Government Departments in many parts of the world.

No 38 Group

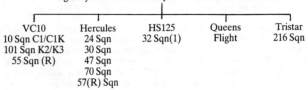

HQ No 38 Group
High Wycombe - Air Transport - Communications - AAR

VC10	Hercules	HS125	Queens	Tristar
10 Sqn C1/C1K	24 Sqn	32 Sqn(1)	Flight	216 Sqn
101 Sqn K2/K3	30 Sqn			
55 Sqn (R)	47 Sqn			
	70 Sqn			
	57(R) Sqn			

Notes: (1) 32 Sqn also has Andover & Gazelle.

Flying Stations

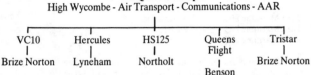

HQ No 38 Group
High Wycombe - Air Transport - Communications - AAR

VC10	Hercules	HS125	Queens Flight	Tristar
Brize Norton	Lyneham	Northolt	Benson	Brize Norton

Air Defence

One of Strike Command's main responsibilities is the United Kingdom Air Defence Region (UKADR). AOC Strike Command delegates day-to-day operational responsibility to the AOC No 11 Group, and the Group's task is to provide early warning of air attack against the UKADR, to provide fighter and missile defences and the associated ground control system, fighter co-ordination with Royal Naval Ships operating in adjacent waters and to maintain the integrity of UK air space in war.

The UK control and reporting centres are linked with other elements of the NATO Air Defence Ground Environment (NADGE) and with the Ballistic Missile Early Warning Systems (BMEWS) station at Fylingdales, Yorkshire, which is networked with the US operated BMEWS at Thule ((Greenland) and Clear (Alaska). By extending high-level radar cover some 3,000 miles across Eastern Europe, Fylingdales would give advance warning of intermediate range ballistic missiles launched against the UK and Western Europe, and of inter-continental ballistic missiles against the North American continent. Fylingdales also tracks satellites and space debris.

The UK Air Defence Region (UKADR) Radar Reporting Network

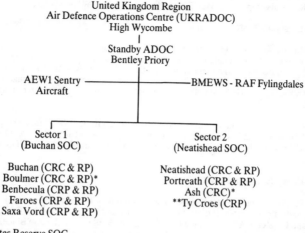

United Kingdom Region
Air Defence Operations Centre (UKRADOC)
High Wycombe

Standby ADOC
Bentley Priory

AEW1 Sentry Aircraft ———————— BMEWS - RAF Fylingdales

Sector 1
(Buchan SOC)

Sector 2
(Neatishead SOC)

Buchan (CRC & RP)
Boulmer (CRC & RP)*
Benbecula (CRP & RP)
Faroes (CRP & RP)
Saxa Vord (CRP & RP)

Neatishead (CRC & RP)
Portreath (CRP & RP)
Ash (CRC)*
**Ty Croes (CRP)

* Denotes Reserve SOC
** Operated by the Royal Danish Air Force

In Reserve - STC Mobile Radar Reserve (144 Signals Unit)

Key:

SOC	-	Sector Operations Centre
CRC	-	Control Reporting Centre
CRP	-	Control Reporting Point
RP	-	Reporting Point

I-UKADGE (Improved- UK Air Defence Ground Environment) is the communications system upon which the air defences depend for their operational effectiveness. The system is fully automated. Computerised data exchange and information from a number of sources such as radars, ships and aircraft is moved around the system on a number of routes to minimise the disruptive effects of enemy action. Generally speaking if a command bunker or radar is rendered inoperable, the system will automatically switch to another node allowing a secure, free and uninterrupted flow of information. ICCS (Integrated Command and Control System) provides the Commanders and air defence staff the information gathered in the system, and UNITER brings together all the nodes on a digital network.

JTIDS (Joint Tactical Information Distribution System) is a secure communications network. The MOD has ordered 60 terminals and the majority of these will equip 2 x Tornado F3 squadrons and the AEW1 Sentry aircraft.

Military Air Traffic Operations

Military Air Traffic Operations (MATO) has Group status within Strike Command and is based at Hillingdon House, Uxbridge. It is co-located with Civil Air Traffic Operations (CATO) under a Joint Field Commander (JFC - Air Commodore - AOC MATO) who is responsible for the joint implementation of National Air Traffic Services (NATS) policy for the control of civil and military aircraft in the UK.

AOCMATO is operationally responsible to the Controller NATS for all military ATC services in UK airspace other than those provided at airfields. MATO is administered by Strike Command in peacetime and controlled by CINCUKAIR in war.

Air Warfare Centre (AWC)

The Air Warfare Centre is responsible for formulating tactical doctrine and conducting operational trials. Formed from the old CTTO, DAW, EWOSE, ORB and OEUs the AWC also maintains liaison with MOD research establishments and industry, and close contact with RAF operational commands as well as with the Royal Navy, Army and Allied air forces.

The Air Warfare Centre is administered by HQ Strike Command, but is responsible jointly to the Assistant Chief of Air Staff, and to the Commander-in-Chief for the conduct of trials, and development of tactics for all Royal Air Force operational aircraft. Branches and locations of the AWC are as follows:

Operational Doctrine (OD&T)	Cranwell & High Wycombe
Tactics (TD&T)	Waddington
Electronic Warfare (EWOS)	Waddington
Operational Analysis (OA)	High Wycombe, Waddington & Cranwell
Operational Testing & Evaluation (OT&E)	Boscombe Down, Conningsby, Odiham & Ash

RAF Command Reorganisation

From April 1st 1994, the old Support Command joins with two major air force departments (AMS & AMP) and then becomes Personnel & Training Command and Logistic Command. The decision to form the two new commands follows the acceptance of the findings of a report by Sir Kenneth Macdonald, who was commissioned by the MOD to study the headquarters and support echelons of the armed forces, with the aim of achieving an overall 20% reduction.

In a recent (1993) interview Air Marshal Sir Michael Alcock (AOCinC designate Logistic Command) stated "By transferring responsibility for maintenance, storage and distribution to HQ Logistic Command and responsibility for training to Personnel and Training Command, it will become possible to dispense with Support Command. Moreover, the greatly improved efficiency arising from the co-location of personnel and logistic staffs within their respective headquarters will enable us to reduce the overall numbers of headquarters staff by 20%.

But, the re-organisation goes much further than this, as it removes a complete layer of management from within the MOD. For example, when I move to take up my appointment as C-in-C Logistics Command in April 1994 the department of the AMSO (Air Member for Supply and Organisation) will transfer with me - somewhat reduced in size, I might add. Similarly, when the Air Member for Personnel moves to become AOC-in-C Personnel and Training Command, he will be accompanied by all the remaining staff from within his MOD department. Consequently, once the re-organisation is completed, the number of Top Level Budget holders will have been reduced from five (AMP, AMSO, C-in-C Strike Command, C-in-C Support Command and C-in-C RAF Germany) down to three (C-in-C Strike Command, C-in-C Logistics Command, C-in-C Personnel and Training Command)".

Sir Michael Alcock further stated that the capital costs for HQ PTC at Innsworth were £38 million and those for the HQ LC complex at Brampton/Wyton were £67 million. In addition, there were personnel relocation and redundancy costs of of approximately £27 million. To offset this total of £132 million, there would be receipts from the sale of facilities that were being closed down, and that savings in the support costs for these facilities would be in the region of £7 million per annum. The reduction in staff numbers and the high costs of operating from London will save £32 million per annum. On this basis Sir Michael, estimates a break even point in four years and an overall saving to the defence budget over the ten year period to 2002 of £237 million.

RAF Personnel & Training Command (RAF PTC)

HQ Personnel and Training Command combines the functions of the AMP (Air Member for Personnel) and the Air Officer Training plus some sections of the planning and administrative staff. The new command therefore controls all personnel aspects ranging from conditions of service, recruiting, training, education, manning, career management, resettlement and pensions.
The new headquarters will also deal with all policy matters relating to Medical, Dental, Legal and Chaplaincy. Final staff numbers will probably be in the areas of 1,500 with a split of about 55% civilians and 45% service personnel.

RAF PTC Organisation

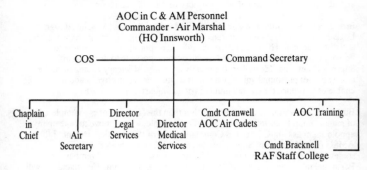

AOC in C & AM Personnel
Commander - Air Marshal
(HQ Innsworth)

COS — Command Secretary

Chaplain in Chief — Air Secretary — Director Legal Services — Director Medical Services — Cmdt Cranwell AOC Air Cadets — AOC Training — Cmdt Bracknell RAF Staff College

Chief of Staff's Branch (COS)

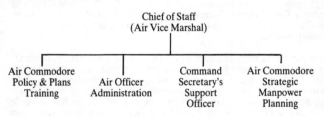

Chief of Staff
(Air Vice Marshal)

Air Commodore Policy & Plans Training — Air Officer Administration — Command Secretary's Support Officer — Air Commodore Strategic Manpower Planning

Air Secretary

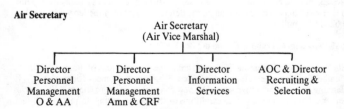

Air Secretary
(Air Vice Marshal)

Director Personnel Management O & AA — Director Personnel Management Amn & CRF — Director Information Services — AOC & Director Recruiting & Selection

42

Director Medical Services

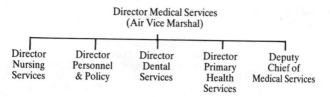

Air Officer Training

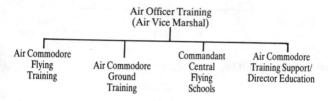

Note: We believe that the Red Arrows will be under the control of AOC Flying Training.

RAF Logistic Command (RAF LC)

Logistics Command will bring together the Defence Agency Maintenance Group, which is responsible for third line repair and overhaul, depot storage and some signals units; the Support Management Group that has been previously located at MOD London, Harrogate and High Wycombe, the recently formed Logistic Support Services organisation which comprises the Stanbridge based Supply Control Division, the Maintenance Analysis and Computing Division and the Central Servicing and and Development Establishment both of which are currently based at Swanton Morley.

The new headquarters located at the Brampton/Wyton complex will have about 4,000 personnel, about 50% of whom will be civilians managing a cash budget of some £1.8 billion, or about half a million pounds per staff member annually. The headquarters "core" staff will number about 200 and the vast majority of the staff will be involved in the direct management and control of maintenance activities such as provisioning, storage, distribution, logistic operations, information systems and communications.

RAF LC Organisation

The following is a guide to what we believe is the organisation for the new RAF Logistic Command.

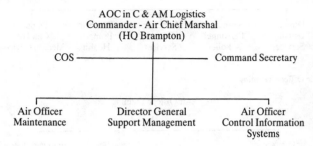

AOC in C & AM Logistics
Commander - Air Chief Marshal
(HQ Brampton)

COS ———————————————— Command Secretary

Air Officer Maintenance — Director General Support Management — Air Officer Control Information Systems

Chief of Staff's Branch (COS)

Chief of Staff
(Air Marshal)
Air Officer Commanding Directly Administerd Units

Air Commodore Policy & Plans — Air Officer Administration — Air Commodore Logistic Support Services — Command Secretary's Support Officer

Air Officer Maintenance

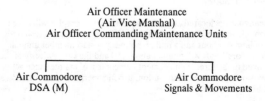

Air Officer Maintenance
(Air Vice Marshal)
Air Officer Commanding Maintenance Units

Air Commodore DSA (M) — Air Commodore Signals & Movements

Director General Support Management

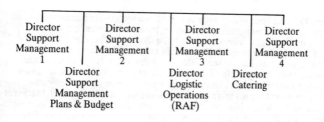

Director General Support Management
(Air Vice Marshal)

Director Support Management 1 — Director Support Management Plans & Budget | Director Support Management 2 | Director Support Management 3 — Director Logistic Operations (RAF) — Director Catering | Director Support Management 4

Air Officer Commanding Signals Units

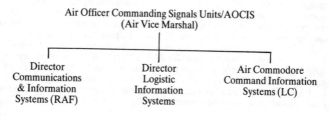

Air Officer Commanding Signals Units/AOCIS
(Air Vice Marshal)

Director Communications & Information Systems (RAF) | Director Logistic Information Systems | Air Commodore Command Information Systems (LC)

Maintenance

The maintenance functions at Logistic Command can be divided into aero systems engineering (those engineering functions concerned with aircraft) signals and movements. RAFLC provides aircraft engineering support for the RAF, and for fixed wing aircraft of the Royal Navy and Army Air Corps. Scheduled major maintenance, rectifications, reconditioning and modification of a wide variety of aircraft are undertaken for tasks beyond the normal capability of operational stations.

Maintenance Units (MUs) also hold reserve stocks of fixed wing aircraft, which they prepare for storage and maintenance against deterioration. Continuous effort is devoted to the improvement of maintenance facilities, the introduction of improved tools and better working methods to increase efficiency and reduce costs.

Work on aircraft is carried out at RAF St Athan. The engineering unit at St Athan, the largest in the RAF, is manned jointly by service personnel and civilians, with an Aircraft Servicing Wing and a General Engineering Wing. The former has been engaged for many years on the maintenance of Harriers, Phantoms and Tornados with the capacity to work on 58 aircraft at any one time.

In July 1992, the engineering facilities at RAF Abingdon were concentrated at St Athan. This move brought responsibility for the major maintenance and modification of Jaguar, Hawk and VC10 aircraft and the Repair and Salvage Squadron, which is responsible for salvaging crashed RAF, Army and Navy fixed wing aircraft in most parts of the world and carries out aircraft recovery for the Department of Transport. In addition to crash recovery, the Repair and Salvage Squadron also sends teams of tradesmen to operational stations to undertake modifications and repairs that are beyond the capacity of unit personnel, but do not necessitate the aircraft being returned to a maintenance unit. In realistic scenarios, aircraft battle damage repair techniques are formulated and tested for all of the British Services, and some 18 other nations have benefited from such training.

No 30 Maintenance Unit (30 MU) at RAF Sealand near Chester, is the main engineering unit for airborne electronic and instrument equipment. Large workshops and test facilities are laid out on production lines to enable the unit to service more than 100,000 items of airborne radio, radar, electrical, instrument and missile engineering equipment a year. The unit also provides a test equipment calibration service and manufactures test equipment, aircraft cables and looms. The RAF Armament Support Unit (RAFASUPU) at RAF Wittering houses the RAF Explosive Ordnance Disposal (EOD) Squadron which is responsible for all aspects of RAF EOD training and trials, as well as actual clearance operations. RAFASUPU also trains aircrew and groundcrew in all aspects of special weapons functions and moves weapons as required.

In addition to the major aircraft engineering tasks, RAF LC repairs almost any kind of equipment when it is expedient and economical to do so. Parachutes, ground equipment, furniture and domestic equipment are typical examples. There are large workshops at each of the Equipment Supply Depots that undertake the modification, repair and servicing of almost any item of equipment that comes from units in an unservicable condition. A considerable sum of money is saved by this repair facility, enabling requirements for scarce equipment to be met more quickly.

Signals

The units controlled by the RAF LC Signals Staffs based at RAF Henlow, are responsible for the support aspects of telecommunications, ground radio repair and signals engineering. The Signal Staff are responsible for operating the RAF element of the Defence Communications Network (DCN) and acts as a consultant to MOD, other RAF Commands and to Allied Air Forces for all aspects of communications. The Signal Staff is also responsible for the Henlow based

Communications-Electronic Multi Disciplinary Group, responsible to the MOD for support authority functions in respect of telegraphic automatic routing equipment, telegraph, ground radio and ground radar equipments for the three services and other organisations.

Communications operating responsibilities fall into four categories. First, there is a large complex of HF transmitter and receiver facilities in the UK, including communications centres with automatic message routing equipment. Operations include those on behalf of Strike Command, the Military Air Traffic Organisation, NATO and the Meteorological Office.

Second, LC operates message relay centres, both automatic and manual and also manages the RAF's General Purpose Telephone network. The RAF has also procured a fixed telecommunications network called Boxer which will save the increasing expense of renting lines from the private sector. Command operating procedures are monitored on all networks to ensure high standards are achieved and maintained. To reduce risk of compromise, all RAF communications facilities designed to carry classified information are checked for communications electrical security by Command staff.

Thirdly, the main operation of the Skynet Satellite Communications System, which offers overseas formations telegraphed, data and speech communications, is controlled by the Command. In February 1994, a contract for some £300 million was awarded for the development, production and delivery of 2 x Skynet 4 Stage 2 military communications satellites. These will replace the existing Skynet satellites as they approach the end of their operational life, and will enter service in 1998. In addition a management service for the NATO 4 series of satellites is provided.

Fourth, the deep maintenance and repair of ground radio and radar equipments are carried out by the Ground Radio Servicing Centre (GRSC) at RAF North Luffenham. This includes radars, radio navigation aids and point-to-point and ground-to-air communications. The Command also provides an antenna systems maintenance service on a world wide basis, embracing the fields of communications, radar and navigation aids. The men required for this highly specialised work are trained by the Command at the Aerial Erector School at RAF Digby.

The Command's responsibilities for electrical engineering range over the entire field of communications equipment, air traffic control and defence radar systems and ground based navigational equipment. They include feasibility studies, project management, design, development, manufacture, refurbishment, installation and commissioning of the majority of communications equipment procured by the MOD(PE).

AOC Signals has a large engineering design staff of engineers, technicians and draughtsmen. Manufacturing resources include a general mechanical engineering and calibration capacity at RAF Henlow and, at RAF Wyton, a facility for the systems design, development and installation of certain airborne signals role equipment.

Supply

The size and composition of the Logistic Command supply units vary according to their respective functions, from equipment supply depots to comparatively small petroleum supply depots. The equipment supply depots hold nearly one and a half million different types of technical and domestic equipment. Quantities vary from a few months to several years consumption, according to whether this item can be replenished quickly or can be bought in economic quantities only when the manufacturer is tooled-up to produce it. The number of different items held in stock is greater, and the variety wider, than would be found in any one civilian firm in the UK. Stocks are at present distributed amongst four large depots located at Stafford, Carlisle, Quedgeley and Chilmark.

Over the years, the technique of stock recording and stock location and the speedy handling of stores items have continually improved. Today the highest priority demands for equipment are fully processed within six hours of their receipt at the depot for delivery throughout the world. This service, which operates 24 hours a day every day of the year, is supported by one of the UK's most powerful computers located at the RAF Supply Control Centre. It is here that a central record of the location and quantity of nearly every item of equipment held throughout the RAF is located.

The equipment supply depots and about 100 stations at home and overseas are linked to the Supply Control Centre. As a result, the computer is able to direct any urgently required item of equipment from the appropriate depot or, if quicker, to be transferred from another RAF station. It also provides accurate consumption information to ensure that the item is purchased in the most cost effective quantities.

Operationally, Logistic Command also supports major force deployments through the Tactical Supply Wing. Based at RAF Stafford, this organisation is equipped to move at very short notice to provide a range of support facilities, including fuel and spares, anywhere in the world.

Overseas Bases

Strike Command has responsibility for all RAF bases overseas, including the units in Germany, the Mediterranean, Far East, North America and Central America (closing in mid-1994).

AHQ Cyprus has Group status within the Strike Command. In Cyprus, there is a resident squadron of Wessex helicopters, some of which support UNFICYP with the remainder in the SAR role, while facilities exist at RAF Akrotiri to support aircraft detached from UK. In addition, an RAF Regiment Squadron is deployed at Akrotiri for airfield defence.

RAF Gibraltar is directly administered by HQ 18 Group. The airfield is operated by the RAF, although there is no resident squadron. Strike Command controls RAF units for administrative and engineering purposes in Hong Kong where there is a squadron of Wessex helicopters. In North America there is a Strike Command detachment at Offutt Air Force Base, Nebraska, to support overseas training detachments, and a permanent unit is established at Goose Bay in Labrador for a similar purpose.

Strike Command also provides a Tornado Air Defence Unit, a flight of Hercules transport/tankers and Sea King and Chinook helicopters in the Falkland Islands. In early 1994, there were Strike Command units operating in support of the United Nations in Saudi Arabia, Bahrain, Turkey and the former Yugoslavia.

During operations and exercises, aircraft often visit overseas airfields where no regular RAF ground handling organisation exists. For this purpose, the Group has a Mobile Air Movement Squadron (MAMS) at RAF Lyneham, which provides teams who are expert in all aspects of loading and unloading aircraft. The MAMS teams log a large number of flying hours annually and are normally on the first aircraft in, and last aircraft out in any major overseas operation, exercise or relief operation.

CHAPTER 4 - FRONT LINE AIRCRAFT

Tornado GR-1

199 x GR1 Accepted into RAF Service
91 x GR1 In squadron service
42 x GR1 With training units
133 x GR1 Available for operations within 24 hours (estimate)
35 x GR1 "Written off" between 12 Jun 79 and 1 Sep 93
31 x GR1 At miscellaneous locations such as BAe, Store-St Athan, DRA etc

In Service With:

ased bird strike protection, a new Aden 25mm cannon and additional electronic countermeasures equipment.

9 Sqn	13 x Tornado GR1	RAF Bruggen
12 Sqn	13 x Tornado GR1	RAF Lossiemouth
14 Sqn	13 x Tornado GR1	RAF Bruggen
17 Sqn	13 x Tornado GR1	RAF Bruggen
31 Sqn	13 x Tornado GR1	RAF Bruggen
617 Sqn	13 x Tornado GR1	RAF Lossiemouth
TWCU (15 R Sqn)*	25 x Tornado GR1	RAF Lossiemouth
TTTE**	17 x Tornado GR1	RAF Cottesmore

* TWCU - Tornado Weapons Conversion Unit.
** TTTE - Trinational Tornado Training Establishment.

Crew 2; Wingspan (open) 13.9m; Wingspan (swept) 8.6m; Height 5.9m; Length 16.7m; Max Weapon Load 7,250kg; Max Take Off Weight 27,900kg; Max Speed Mach 2.2 (1452 mph); Max Ferry Range approx 3,900kms; Armament 2 x 27mm Mauser Cannon, 3 x weapon points under fuselage, 4 x weapon points under wings; Engines 2 x Turbo-Union RB 199-34R Turbofans; Required Runway Length approx 900m.

The Tornado GR-1 is an aircraft jointly developed by the UK, West Germany and Italy under a collaborative agreement and manufactured by a consortium of companies formed under the name of Panavia. The Tornado is the most numerous and important aircraft in the RAF inventory and the GR-1 operates in the strike/attack and reconnaissance roles. The first prototype flew in 1974 and the first RAF Squadron equipped with the GR-1 became operational in 1982. The GR-1 is capable of of carrying both nuclear and conventional weapons at tree-top height, in all weathers, by day or by night. It has a very advanced terrain following radar and sophisticated electronic countermeasures which assist in penetrating hostile airspace. For self-defence a 27mm cannon and Sidewinder missiles are carried. The Tornado GR-1A is the reconnaissance version of the aircraft, and the GR-1B is an aircraft modified to allow the Sea Eagle missile to be used to its full capability.

During the Gulf War Tornado GR1s were amongst the first aircraft in action from 17th January. Equipped with JP233 airfield denial weapons, 1,000 pound bombs and ALARM anti-radar missiles, GR1s attacked a number of the Iraqi Air Force's huge airfields. During the first week of operations the majority of the GR1 sorties were flown at low level and at night, an environment in which few other aircraft could operate.

By the end of the first week of operations the Iraqi Air Force was either in hiding in Iran or was trapped on damaged airfields. The overwhelming success of the offensive counter-air campaign against the Iraqi airfields created the opportunity to change Tornado tactics and, for the next three weeks, the GR1 force flew both day and night missions against a variety of interdiction targets, whilst continuing interval bombardment of Iraqi targets. With the air threat neutralised, the Tornado GR1 could now operate at medium level, above the reach of anti-aircraft artillery and using ballistic free fall 1,000 pound bombs.

The deployment of a squadron of Buccaneer aircraft equipped with Pavespike laser designators enabled the Tornado GR1s to use Laser Guided Bombs (LGBs) with great precision during daylight raids on interdiction and airfield targets. The GR1s capability was further enhanced with the deployment of a small number of aircraft fitted with the new Thermal Imaging Airborne Laser Designator (TIALD) which gave the Tornado GR1s a precision night attack capability. The final three weeks of the air war saw the Tornado GR1 force concentrating almost exclusively on day and night precision attacks dropping LGBs from medium altitude.

A total of six GR1s were lost in action, five of which were involved in low or medium level attacks with 1,000 pound bombs and one that was flying a low level JP233 mission. During the war, the Tornado GR1 force flew 1,500 operational sorties divided almost equally between offensive counter air targets such as airfields and air defence sites, and interdiction targets such as bridges. Between them, Tornado GR1 and Jaguar GR1A's dropped some 100 x JP233 airfield denial weapons, 5,000 x 1,000 pound bombs, 1,000 x LGBs, 100 x ALARM missiles and 700 x Air to Ground Rockets onto Iraqi positions. The RAF deployed 48 x GR1 in the area during hostilities.

The first aircraft of the Tornado GR4 MLU version (mid life update) took off from British Aerospace (Wharton) for a 90 minute flight during June 1993. The development contract for the MLU programme was signed with BAe in 1989 and includes introducing new equipment and updated avionics into the basic Tornado GR1 airframe. In addition, lessons from the Gulf War have been incorporated in the programme and it is believed that an improved thermal imaging laser designator pod and integrated global positioning system have been included. Panavia's proposal for the entire MLU programme will probably be presented to the UK MOD at the end of 1994. Funds are believed to have been allocated for the update of 161 aircraft at a total cost of £657 million (just over £4 million per aircraft) with peak years of expenditure between 1996 and 2000.

Panavia recently announced a proposal to build a "technology demonstrator" aircraft which would investigate and model the weapons and technology for air force requirements during the period 2030 and beyond. This "technology demonstrator" could be the catalyst for the development of an aircraft that would be a potential replacement for the Tornado GR1/GR4 in RAF service, and would have sales potential amongst all of the European Community nations.

Tornado GR1A

28 x GR1A Accepted in RAF service
26 x GR1A In Squadron service
2 x GR1A "Written off" on 9 Jan 90 and 19 Jan 91.

In Service With:

2 Sqn	13 x Tornado GR1A	RAF Marham
13 Sqn	13 x Tornado GR1	RAF Marham

The Tornado GR1A is the Recce version of the Tornado and has what the RAF describes as "a unique day/night low level reconnaissance capability". During the Gulf War, six Tornado GR1A aircraft, usually flying in pairs at night and at low level, flew some 140 operational sorties.

Tornado F3

170 x F3 Accepted into RAF Service
90 x F3 Available for Immediate Operational Service.
24 x F3 With Training Units
2 x F3 "Written Off" on 21 Jul 89 & 21 Oct 93
40 x F3 In miscellaneous locations such as BAe, St Athan, etc

Note: In early 1994 Italy leased 24 x Tornado F3 from the UK to bridge the gap until the Eurofighter enters service.

Crew 2; Wingspan (open) 13.9m; Wingspan (swept) 8.6m; Height 5.9m; Length 18.6m; Max Take Off Weight 27,900kg; Max Speed Mach 2.2 (1452 mph); Armament 1 x 27mm Mauser Cannon, 4 x Sky Flash; 4 x AIL 9L Sidewinder; Engines 2 x Turbo-Union RB 199-34R-Mk104 Turbofans; Intercept Radius 1,850 km (subsonic) or 550 kms (supersonic).

In Service With:

5 Sqn	13 x Tornado F3	RAF Coningsby
11 Sqn	13 x Tornado F3	RAF Leeming
25 Sqn	13 x Tornado F3	RAF Leeming
29 Sqn	13 x Tornado F3	RAF Coningsby
43 Sqn	16 x Tornado F3	RAF Leuchars
111 Sqn	16 x Tornado F3	RAF Leuchars
56 Sqn (R) OCU	24 x Tornado F3	RAF Coningsby
1435 Flight	Tornado F3	RAF MPA (Falklands)

(1) 23 Sqn Disbands on 1 April 1994.
(2) Figures include AE (air establishment) and IUR (in use reserve aircraft).

The Tornado F3 is armed with 4 x semi-recessed Sky Flash, 4 x Sidewinder AIM 9L missiles and a single Mauser 27mm cannon and has about 80% commonality with the Tornado GR1. The main difference is the extended fuselage, longer range air intercept Foxhunter Radar (replacing the terrain following/ground mapping radar of the Tornado GR1) and the armament. Extension of the fuselage provides additional space for avionics and an extra 900 litres of fuel.

The F3 was designed to meet the RAF's commitment for the air defence of the extensive UK Air Defence Region (UKADR). The aircraft has a long range autonomous capability that enables operations to be conducted some 350 nm away from bases in bad weather, in an ECM environment and operating against multiple-targets at high or low level, which can be engaged at distances in excess of 20 nm. With tanker support the Tornado F3 Combat Air Patrol (CAP) time is increased from 2 hrs and 30mins to a loiter time of several hours.

The Air Defence Variant (ADV) of the Tornado from which the F3 was developed flew for the first time in October 1979. The F3 will almost certainly stay in service until it is replaced by the European Fighter Aircraft (EFA) during the early part of the next century.

RAF Tornado F3s were sent to the Gulf in August 1990 and by the end of hostilities on the 28th Feburary 1991, 18 x F3 aircraft had flown some 2,500 sorties during their deployment including 700 sorties during the period of hostilities. During 1993, the RAF has participated in NATO operations to enforce a No-Fly Zone over Bosnia as part of Operation Deny Flight. By August 1993, 8 x F-3 aircraft had been deployed to the airbase at Gioia del Colle in Italy and had flown over 250 sorties.

There are believed to be 18 x Tornado F2 in store at RAF St Athan. These F2 differ from the F3 in that the F3 versions have uprated engines, automatic wing sweep and manoeuvering systems and improved avionics. We believe that plans to uprate these F2 to F3 standard may well have been overtaken by events.

Note: The Tornado F3 lost on 21 Oct 93 was on a routine training sortie over County Durham, flying at 2,000 feet and 300 knots. The aircraft suffered a major fuselage fuel leak and an associated engine flame out. Both crew members ejected safely.

Tornado in World Service

	GR1/IDS	F2/F3/ADV	ECR/GR1A/Recce
UK	199	170	26
Germany	302		- 36
Italy	70	24 (leased from UK)	-
Saudi Arabia	48	24	-

Jaguar GR Mark 1A and T Mk 2A

GR1A   -   77 Taken into service
9 "Written Off"
43 In Squadron Service
25 At various locations, storage - OCU, Shawbury, A&EE etc

T2A   -   18 Taken into service
2 "Written Off"
16 In Service

In Service With:

6 Sqn	14 x Jaguar GR1A 3 x Jaguar T2A	RAF Coltishall
41 Sqn	14 x Jaguar GR1A 2 x Jaguar T2A	RAF Coltishall
54 Sqn	15 x Jaguar GR1A 2 x Jaguar T2A	RAF Coltishall
16 Sqn (R) OCU	10 x Jaguar (GR1A & T2A)	RAF Lossiemouth

Crew (GR 1A) 1 (T Mark 2A) 2; Length (GR 1A) 15.52m (T Mark 2A) 16.42m; Wingspan 8.69m; Height 4.89m; All Up Operational Weight approx 11,000kgs; Max Speed 1,350 km/ph(1056mph) Armament (GR 1A) 2 x 30mm Aden Cannon (T Mark 2A) 1 x 30mm Aden Cannon, Martel, Sea Eagle, BL 755, bombs and rockets; Engines 2 x Rolls-Royce Turbomeca Adour Mk 104s.

The Anglo-French Jaguar entered RAF service in 1973, the first aircraft being delivered to the Operational Conversion Unit at RAF Lossiemouth in Scotland. Powered by two Rolls Royce/Turbomeca Ardour turbofan engines, the Jaguar was built by the BAC/Breguet consortium Sepecat. Two RAF versions remain in service the GR1A and the T2A.

The Jaguar carries an impressive weapons load beneath four wing pylons and a centre line pylon. Weapons include cluster bombs, 1,000 pound retarded and free fall bombs and other bombs, rockets and missiles. The aircraft carries 30mm cannon internally and for self defence the GR1A has a comprehensive suite of electronic countermeasures, a radar warning receiver and overwing Sidewinder missiles.

The most impressive feature of the Jaguar is the highly advanced and automated navigation and attack system. The "chisel" nose contains the Laser Ranging and Marked Target Seeker and, in addition to the on-board computer, there is a moving map display and a head-up display.
The pilot of a Jaguar can feed the data for his mission into the computer and all of the relevant information required for pin-point attack is supplied on the head-up display, showing him where the target is located and where to release the particular weapons being carried.

During the Gulf War, the RAF deployed a Squadron of 12 x Jaguar GR1A to the region. This squadron was employed on a variety of battlefield interdiction (BAI) and close air support (CAS) missions. Although only operating during daylight, the Jaguars displayed great versatility and flew over 600 operational sorties without loss. In addition to their operations over land, the Jaguars were also successful in destroying Iraqi patrol boats and landing craft in the Gulf. Jaguars also flew tactical reconnaissance sorties. Tornado GR1 and Jaguar GR1A's dropped some 100 x JP233 airfield denial weapons, 5,000 x 1,000 pound bombs, 1,000 x LGBs, 100 x ALARM missiles and 700 x Air to Ground Rockets onto Iraqi positions.

Current MOD plans assume that the Jaguar will start to withdraw from service during 2004.

Harrier

GR5/7   -   96 Accepted into Service
            6 "Written Off"
            40 In Squadron Service
            50 At Various Locations OCU, AAEE, DRA, Store etc.

In Service With:

1 Sqn	14 x Harrier GR7	RAF Wittering
3 Sqn	13 x Harrier GR7	RAF Laarbruch
4 Sqn	13 x Harrier GR7	RAF Laarbruch
20 Sqn (R) OCU*	16 x Harrier	RAF Wittering

* There appear to be a mix of aircraft at the OCU. We believe that there could be Harrier GR3, GR5/7 and up to 10 x Harrier T4.

Crew (GR 5/7) 1; (T Mark 4 & 4A) 2; Length (GR 5/7) 14m; Length (T Mark 4 & 4A) 17m; Wingspan (normal) 9.3m; Height (GR 5/7) 3.45m; Height (T Mark 4 & 4A) 4.17m; Max Speed 1083 km/ph (673mph) at sea level; All Up Operational Weight approx 13,494kgs; Armament 2 x 30mm Aden guns, 4 x wing weapon pylons and 1 x underfuselage weapon pylon, conventional or cluster bombs; Engine 1 x Rolls-Royce Pegasus 11-21; Ferry Range 5,382 kms (3,310 miles) with 4 x drop tanks.

Capable of taking off and landing vertically, the Harrier is not tied to airfields with long concrete runways but can be dispersed to sites in the field close to the forward edge of the battle area. The normal method of operation calls for a short take off and vertical landing (STOVL), as a short ground roll on take off enables a greater weapon load to be carried.

The Harrier GR3 was the mark of the aircraft that was taken into service in large numbers starting in 1969.

The Harrier GR5 entered service in 1988 with the intention of replacing all of the RAF's GR3's on a one for one basis. However, the GR5 has been upgraded to the GR7, which in turn entered service in June 1990. All three of the operational Harrier squadrons have been equipped with the GR7 and all of the GR3s and GR5s have either been upgraded or withdrawn from service.

The differences in the GR5 and the GR7 are mainly in the avionics. The GR7 is equipped with the Forward Looking Infra Red (FLIR) equipment which, when combined with the night vision goggles (NVGs) that the pilot will wear, gives the GR7 a night, low level, poor weather capability. There are small differences in the cockpit layout of the two aircraft including layout and internal lighting standards. In most other respects, the GR7 is similar to the GR5.

The GR5/7 offers many advantages over the GR3. It posesses the capability to carry approximately twice the weapon load over the same radius of action, or the same weapon load over a much increased radius. In addition it carries a comprehensive ECM (Electronic Counter Measures) suite which can operate in the passive or active mode and will greatly enhance the GR5/7s chances of survival in today's high threat environment. The GR5/7 also has an inertial navigation system that is significantly more effective than that of the GR3.

The cockpit of the GR5/7 has been completely revised. The raising of the cockpit in relation to the aircraft has vastly improved the pilot's lookout. Furthermore, the design has incorporated the principle of Hands-On-Throttle and Stick (HOTAS). To aid systems management Cathode Ray Tube (CRT) displays are much in evidence for the display of the FLIR image, moving map, systems status and flying instruments displays. Each CRT has numerous multi-function reprogrammable keys for each function selection, again aiding systems management.

The LRMTS of the GR3 has been replaced with the Angle Rate Bombing System (ARBS) as the primary weapon aiming system. The ARBS incorporates a Dual Mode Tracker, either TV colour contrasts or laser spot tracker. The GR5/7 has an increased wing area, improved aerodynamic qualities and the incorporation of Leading Edge Root Extensions which all combine to give the GR5/7 much improved manouverability over that of the GR3. However, the GR5/7 maintains its ability to vector the engine's thrust in forward flight (VIFF), again increasing manouverability.

The GR5/7 was derived from the McDonnell Douglas/British Aerospace AV-8B. Noteworthy changes include the addition of a moving map display, Martin Baker ejection seat, increased bird strike protection, a new Aden 25mm cannon and additional electronic countermeasures equipment.

The T4A is a 2 seat trainer version of the aircraft. The Fleet Air Arm version of this aircraft is the FRS1/2. A total of 13 x Harrier T10 advanced trainers are on order and deliveries should commence in 1994.

Nimrod

45	Accepted into Service
1	"Written Off" - November 1980
11	AEW Aircraft Scrapped
26	Kinloss Air Wing
3	51 Sqn EW
4	Various Locations Including Storage.

In Service With:

Maritime Reconnaissance

120 Sqn	7 x Nimrod MR2P	RAF Kinloss
201 Sqn	7 x Nimrod MR2P	RAF Kinloss
206 Sqn	7 x Nimrod MR2P	RAF Kinloss
42 Sqn (R) OCU	5 x Nimrod MR2P	RAF Kinloss

Note: This group of units is known as the Kinloss Air Wing. We are reasonably certain that there are approximately 26 aircraft in this group at any one time. Aircraft are shown as being allocated to squadrons for ease of accounting - real numbers may change almost daily.

Electronic Warfare

51 Sqn	3 x Nimrod R1	RAF Wyton (Waddington 1995)

Characteristics MR2P:

Crew 12; Length 38.60m; Span 35m; Height 9.08m; Max Speed 926km ((575mph); Max All Up Weight 87,090 kgs; Endurance 12 hrs; Ferry Range 9265 kms; Armament Harpoon, Sidewinder, Sea Eagle, 9 x Mark 46 or Stingray Torpedoes, bombs; Engines 4 x Rolls Royce Spey RB 168-20 Mark 250 Turbofans.

There are currently two variants of the Nimrod in RAF service. The first is the MR Mark 2P, which has been developed for long range maritime patrol. Its long ferry range enables the crew to moniter seaspace far to the north of Iceland and up to 4,000 kms out into the Western Atlantic. With AAR (Air to Air Refueling), its range and endurance is greatly extended. The MR Mark 2 is a very lethal submarine killer which carries the most up to date sensors and data procesing equipment linked to the weapon systems. In addition to weapons and sonarbouys, a searchlight mounted in the starboard wing pod can be used for search and rescue (SAR) operations.

The second version is the R Mark 1 which is specially fitted out for the gathering of electronic intelligence and only three are known to be in service. This is a highly secret aircraft that has been in RAF service since 1971 and about which little is known except that has been spotted on patrol over the Baltic Sea.

Nimrod is a development of the basic Comet No 4C airframe which dates from the late 1940's. Both the current variants are descended from the original Nimrod MR Mark 1 version (first flight May 1967) that is no longer in service. Nimrod is a outstanding maritime patrol system and we are sure that, given the correct technical enhancements at frequent intervals, the aircraft will remain in service past the turn of the century.

The recently issued (1993) Staff Requirement (Air) 420, the "Replacement Maritime Patrol Aircraft" due in service in 1999, outlines a requirement for an aircraft with long endurance, anti-submarine capability, very long range (over the horizon) targeting and a search and rescue capability. Some possible airframe types to fit this requirement could range from civilian conversions of the Airbus or Boeing airliners, Atlantique 2, P-3 Orion, a maritime version of the FLA or a straight Nimrod upgrade.

Sentry AEW1

7 Accepted into RAF Service

In Service With:

| 8 Sqn | 7 x Sentry AEW1 | RAF Waddington |

Crew; 5 x Flight Crew and 13 x Mission Crew; Length 46.61m; Wingspan 44.42m; Height 12.73m; All Up Operational Weight 147,400kgs; Max Speed 853 km/ph (530 mph); Patrol Endurance 6 hours (can be enhanced by AAR); (Ferry Range 3,200 kms; Engines 4 x CFM-56-2A-3 ; Armament provision for self-defence air-to-air missiles.

Deliveries of the RAF's new Airborne Early Warning (AEW) aircraft, the Sentry AEW1, commenced in March 1991 and delivery of all seven airframes was complete in early 1992. These seven aircraft are of the same type as the 18 delivered to the multi-national NATO early warning force between 1982/ 1985. All are equipped with the Joint Tactical Information Distribution System (JTIDS) and a 665,360 word memory secure communication system.

Powered by four CFM 56-2A-3 engines, the Sentry is designed to cruise at 29,000 feet whilst detecting air and surface contacts with its AN/APY-2 surveillance radar. Information is then transmitted back to interceptor aircraft and, ground, air and ship based units using a wide variety of digital data links.

Almost certainly the most complex airborne system yet to enter RAF service, the Sentry carries a crew of 17 which includes 5 x flight deck crew, 9 x mission crew and 3 x airborne technicians.

Canberra

In Service With:

| 39 Sqn (1PRU) | 7 x Canberra PR9 | RAF Marham |
| 360 Sqn | 9 x Canberra T17 & T17A | RAF Wyton* |

* EW Training/Radar Calibration will be civilianised when 360 Sqn disbands in October 1994.

Crew 2-3; Length 19.96m; Wingspan 19.49m; Height 4.75m; All Up Operational Weight 24,925kg; Max Speed 871 km/ph (541 mph); Service Ceiling 14,630m (48,000ft); Range 1,295kms (with full bomb load); Armament capable of carrying 3,269kg of bombs and rockets plus guns and self-defence air-to-air missiles.

The Canberra is an aircraft that first flew in 1949 and since that date aircraft of twelve different marks have been exported to 11 air forces worldwide. The most numerous of these was the Canberra B2, of which over 400 were manufactured.

The last Canberra B2 made its final flight at RAF Wyton on 7th July 1993. This aircraft WJ731 was first brought into service in November 1953 and by the time it retired, had flown 7,392 hours (306 days) and made some 6,333 landings.

The RAF retains Canberras for photographic reconnaissance, EW training and radar calibration, although the EW training and radar calibration role, is due to be civilianised in 1994.

Hawk

85 x Hawk T1 Accepted Into Service
91 x Hawk T1A Accepted Into Service
17 x Hawk T1 "Written Off"
7 x Hawk T1A "Written Off"
68 x Hawk T1 In Various Locations
84 x Hawk T1A In Various Locations

In Service With:

19 Sqn (R)	25 x Hawk T1/T1A	(7 FTS)	RAF Chivenor (1)
74 Sqn (R)	21 x Hawk T1/T1A	(4 FTS)	RAF Valley
92 Sqn (R)	22 x Hawk T1/T1A	(7 FTS)	RAF Chivenor
100 Sqn	12 x Hawk T1/T1A		RAF Finningley
234 Sqn (R)	20 x Hawk T1/T1A	(4 FTS)	RAF Valley (2)
Red Arrows	12 x Hawk T1/T1A		RAF Scampton
Station Flight	2 x Hawk T1		RAF St Athan
Central Flying School	12 x Hawk T1/T1A		RAF Scampton

(1) 7 FTS at Chivenor ceases operations in October 1994. Flying and training functions concentrated at RAF Valley.
(2) 234 Sqn (R) will become 208 Sqn (R) on 1 April 1994, when the current 208 Sqn based at Lossiemouth and equipped with Buccaneer disbands.

Crew 2; Span 9.39m; Length 11.17m; Height 3.99m; Weight Empty 3647kg; Max Take Off Weight 8569kg; Max Speed 1038 kph (645 mph) at 3355m; Combat Radius 556 kms (345 miles); Engine 1 x 2359 kg thrust Rolls Royce/Turbomecca Adour Mk 151 turbofan; Armament 30mm Aden cannon, 2 x AIM-9L Sidewinder plus assorted bombs and rockets.

The Hawk first flew in 1974, and entered RAF service two years later both as an advanced flying trainer and a weapons training aircraft. It has an economical Adour engine - an un-reheated version of the same turbofan powering the Jaguar.

Hawks are used to teach pilots destined for the "fast-jet" squadrons, operational tactics, air to air and air to ground firing, air combat and low level operating procedures. As a weapons trainer the Hawk is armed with an Aden cannon carried beneath the fuselage, and rocket pods or practice bombs can be fitted to underwing pylons. To fulfil its mobilisation role as a fighter aircraft, the Hawk carries a 30mm Aden cannon and two Sidewinder air-to-air missiles and is designated T1A. By 1995 about 50 Hawks will be equipped for the air defence mobilisation role.

The Hawk is a strong and rugged aircraft designed to cut training and maintenance costs. The aircraft has a long fatigue life to ensure a service career throughout the 1990s and beyond.

Eurofighter 2000

The Eurofighter 2000 (formerly EFA) is a highly agile, single seat, STOL capable aircraft optimised for air superiority/air defence and ground attack roles. The aircraft is part of a European co-production programme with the major manufacturing firms involved being British Aerospace, DASA, CASA and Alenia. British Aerospace (BAe) are responsible for the front fuselage, foreplanes, starboard leading edge flaps and flaperons; BAe/CASA the starboard wing; Alenia the port wing; DASA the centre fuselage, fin and rudder; Alenia/CASA the rear fuselage.

The first flight of the Eurofighter 2000 is scheduled for April 15th 1994 from Manching Air base near Munich in Germany, and such is the importance of this project, that the Defence Ministers of the four nations that should eventually become users of the aircraft, Germany, Italy, Spain and the United Kingdom will all be present.

Eurofighter is designed to carry 6 x medium range and 2 x close range air to air missiles. The aircraft has 13 x store stations and an internal gun fitted on the starboard side. No modifications will be necessary to carry "smart" weapons and 3 stations can carry external fuel pods. The Defensive Aids Sub-System (DASS) equipment is carried in 2 x wing pods that are an integral part of the wing. The aircraft will weigh about 37,000 lbs (approx 16,800 kgs) and be able to operate from a 500 metre strip.

The aircraft is designed to operate with a minumum of ground support requiring only 4 fitters to change an engine in 45 minutes, and a standard of nine man/servicing hours per flying hour as opposed to from 20 to 60 hours for other modern combat aircraft.

During 1995, the four nations in the Eurofighter consortium will announce figures for their requirement. The current (early 1994) RAF plan is to procure 250 Eurofighters that are to replace the Tornado F3's and Jaguars. If all goes to plan, the first aircraft should enter RAF service in the year 2000. The UK MODs latest estimate is that some 300 British companies are in the Eurofighter supply chain, and that the project is currently supporting about 9,000 jobs. This figure is expected to rise to about 28,000 UK jobs during the peak production years.

CHAPTER 5 - SUPPORT AIRCRAFT

VC-10

> 39 Accepted Into RAF Service
> 10 Mark C1
> 3 Mark C1K
> 5 Mark K2
> 4 Mark K3
> 5 Mark K4 (Under conversion)
> 12 In Various Locations (Some Scrapped)

In Service With:

10 Sqn	10 x VC-10 C1/C1K	RAF Brize Norton
101 Sqn	9 x VC-10 K2/K3 (AAR)	RAF Brize Norton

Crew 4; Carries 150 passengers or 78 medical litters; Height 12.04m; Span 44.55m; Length 48.36m; Max Speed (425 mph); Range 7596kms; All Up Operational Weight 146,513kgs; Engines 4 x Rolls Royce Conway turbofans.

The VC-10 is a fast transport aircraft which is the backbone of Strike Command's long-range capability, providing flexibility and speed of deployment for British Forces. This multi-purpose aircraft can be operated in the troop transport, freight and aeromedical roles in addition to maintaining scheduled air services.

During early 1993, the first VC10's for modification to C1K status were modified by FR Aviation of Bournmouth. The new mark of aircraft will have a dual role of two point air to air refueling and air transport. In time all of 10 Sqns aircraft will be modified in this way.

The VC-10 carries a flight deck crew of four - captain, co-pilot, navigator and engineer - and has a flight deck seat for an additional supernumerary crew member. Normal cabin staff are two air loadmasters and two air stewards. On scheduled services up to 126 passengers are carried. Under the floor of the aircraft are two large holds which can carry up to 8.5 tons of freight. If necessary, the aircraft can be converted for use as a freighter or an air ambulance when 78 stretcher cases can be carried.

Five standard VC-10s (K Mark 2 - ex British Airways) and four super VC-10's (K Mark 3 - ex East African Airways) have been converted for use as refuelling tankers. Major changes from the civil transport role include two underwing refuelling pods, a centre line hose drum unit, a refueling probe, additional fuel tanks in the former passenger cabin and a CCTV system to permit the crew to moniter air-to-air (AAR) refueling operations.

C-130 Hercules

> 66 Accepted into Service
> 5 "Written Off"
> 7 Miscellaneous Locations
> 54 Lyneham Tactical Wing (LTW)

In Service With:

24 Sqn	13 x Hercules C1P/C3P/C1K	RAF Lyneham
30 Sqn	13 x Hercules C1/C3/C1K	RAF Lyneham
47 Sqn	11 x Hercules C1/C3	RAF Lyneham
70 Sqn	12 x Hercules	RAF Lyneham
57 Sqn (R) OCU	5 x Hercules	RAF Lyneham

Note: The LTW appears to have a total of 54 aircraft. The squadron totals are given as a guide to what we believe are the average aircraft figures per squadron and the OCU at any one time. Aircraft at the LTW appear to be 23 x C1, 28 x C3 and 3 x C1K.

Crew 5; Capacity 92 troops or 62 paratroops or 74 medical litters or 19,686kgs of freight; Length 29.78m; Span 40.41m; Height 11.66m; Weight Empty 34,287kgs; Max Load 45,093kgs; Max speed 618 km/ph (384mph); Service Ceiling 13,075m; Engines 4 x Allison T-56A-15 turboprops.

The Hercules C1 is the workhorse of the RAF transport fleet. It has proved to be a versatile and rugged aircraft, primarily intended for tactical operations, including troop carrying, paratrooping, supply dropping and aeromedical duties. The Hercules can operate from short unprepared airstrips, but also posesses the the endurance to mount long range strategic lifts if required. The aircraft is a derivative of the C-130E used by the United States Air Force, but is fitted with British Avionic equipment, a roller-conveyor system for heavy air-drops and with more powerful engines. The crew of five includes, pilot, co-pilot, navigator, air engineer and air loadmaster.

As a troop carrier, the Hercules can carry 92 fully armed men, while for airborne operations 62 paratroops can be dispatched in two simultaneous "sticks" through the fuselage side doors. Alternatively, 40 paratroops can jump from the rear loading ramp. As an air ambulance the aircraft can accommodate 74 stretchers.

Freight loads that can be parachuted from the aircraft include: 16 x 1 ton containers or 4 x 8,000 pound platforms or 2 x 16,000 pound platforms or 1 x platform of 30,000 pounds plus. Amongst the many combinations of military loads that can be carried in an air-landed operation are: 3 x Ferret scout cars plus 30 passengers or 2 x Land Rovers and 30 passengers or 2 x Gazelle helicopters.

Of the original 66 C1 aircraft, some 31 have been given a fuselage stretch producing the Mark C3. The C3 "stretched version" provides an additional 37% more cargo space. Refueling probes have been fitted above the cockpit of both variants and some have received radar warning pods under the wing tips. One aircraft, designated Mark W2, is a special weather version and is located at the DRA Farnborough.

RAF Hercules are currently assisting in airlifting aid in support of UN operations in many areas of the world. For example, working from a forward airhead at Ancona on the eastern coast of Italy, a detachment of 38 officers and men with a single Hercules from 47 Sqn, averaged almost three flights a day for the year 3 July 1992 - 3 July 1993. Over 900 sorties lifted more than 19 million pounds of freight into Sarajevo. The aircraft were flown by six crews on a two week rotation from RAF Lyneham.

Current plans appear to be for the replacement of the RAF's ageing 1960s Hercules fleet during the next ten years. Lockheed are believed to be offering the RAF their improved C-130J which has improved engines, a new glass cockpit with flat screen displays and a two man crew. The first test and demonstrator aircraft are expected to be flying in September 1995 with production models available from the middle of 1996.

What the RAF will actually procure is still the subject of much speculation. It would appear that the purchase of approximately 30 x C-130Js (or refurbishment of the in-service C-130Cs to a new K standard) is an option before the end of the 1990s. After that, both the C-130J and the FLA (Future Large Aircraft) will almost certainly be contenders for the second batch of 30 replacements in the early part of the next decade. The FLA which will be built by the Rome based Euroflag Consortium, will probably be ready for service from about 2004 and could be capable of carrying a maximum payload of 30 tons as opposed to the 20 tons of the C-130J. British Aerospace is a member of Euroflag.

The most commonly quoted argument in favour of the FLA is that this aircraft could carry a 25 ton payload over a distance of 4,000kms. Thus it is argued that a fleet of 40 x FLA could carry a UK Brigade to the Gulf within 11.5 days, as opposed to the 28.5 days required to make a similar deployment with 40 x C-130s.

Whatever happens in the longer term, we are sure that examples of the C-130 which first flew as the US YC-130 prototype in 1954, and entered RAF service in the late 1960s will still be flying from RAF airfields for some considerable time during the next century.

Over 1,000 x C-130 have been manufactured. National users of the aircraft are:

Abu Dhabi 6; Algeria 17; Argentina 7; Australia 12; Belgium 12; Boliva 2; Brazil 8; Cameroon 3; Canada 14; Chad 2; Chile 2; Colombia 2; Denmark 3; Dubai 1; Ecuador 3; Egypt 25; France 12; Gabon 1; Greece 12; Indonesia 11; Iran 32; Israel 10; Italy 14; Japan 15; Jordan 4; South Korea 12; Libya 16; Malaysia 10; Morocco 17; New Zealand 5; Niger 2; Nigeria 9; Norway 6; Oman 3; Philippines 3; Portugal 6; Saudi Arabia 49; Singapore 6; Spain 13; Sudan 6; Sweden 5; Taiwan 13; Thailand 12; Tunisia 2; United Kingdom 66; Venezuela 8; Yemen 2; Zaire 7. The United States Air Force operates 427 x C-130s of various marks and the United States Navy another 39.

Tristar

> 9 Accepted Into Service
> 9 In Squadron Service

In Service With:

216 Sqn   9 x Tristar K1/KC1/C2   RAF Brize Norton

Crew 3; Passengers 265 and 35,000 pounds of freight; Length 50.05m; Height 16.87m; Span 47.35m; Max Speed 964 km/ph (600mph); Range 6,000 miles (9,600 kms); Engines 3 x 22,680kgs thrust Rolls Royce RB 211-524B4 turbofans.

The Tristar K1 and KC1 are strategic tanker conversions of the Lockheed L-1011-500 Tristar commercial airliner. The Tristars in RAF service have additional underfloor fuel tanks, twin hose drum units in the rear fuselage, a refuelling probe and a CCTV system to permit the crew to moniter air to air refueling operations.

The Tristar K1 can also be fitted with up to 204 passenger seats for the trooping role. The Tristar KC1 tanker/freight aircraft have a large 140 x 102 inch, cargo door and a roller conveyor system capable of accepting up to 20 cargo pallets or seating for up to 196 passengers. Linked pallets can be used to permit the carriage of vehicles.

The K1 and the KC1 have a flight deck crew of three - captain, co-pilot and flight engineer - and provision for two supernumerary crew members on the flight deck. A loadmaster and air stewards are also carried when the aircraft is operating in the air transport role. Both Tristar variants have have seating for up to 12 supernumerary crew at the forward end of each aircraft.

Also in service is the Tristar C2. This aircraft can carry 265 passengers and 35,000 pounds of freight over ranges in excess of 4,000 miles. It is planned to give these aircraft a tanker capability by fitting two wing refuelling pods.

The Tristar normally cruises at 525mph and with a payload of 50,000 pounds has a range in excess of 6,000 miles. The aircraft entered service in early 1986 with No 216 Sqn which reformed at RAF Brize Norton on 1 Nov 1984.

During 1993, 2 x Tristar K1's deployed to the Italian Air Force Base at Malpensa to support fighter aircraft in enforcing the Bosnian No-Fly Zone as part of the UN Operation Deny Flight. The Tristars flew their first operational mission on June 11th supporting the 8 x RAF F3 Tornados based at the Italian base at Gioia del Colle. The Tristar detachment at Malpensa cosists of about 70 officers and men.

BAe 146 Series 100

3 Accepted Into Service

In Service With:

The Queen's Flight   3 x BAe 146 Series 100   RAF Benson

Crew 2; Length 26.2m; Span 26.3m; Height 8.61m; Max Speed 723 km/ph (351mph); Engines 4 x Avco Lycoming ALF 502R-5 turbofans.

Three BAe 146 Series 100 aircraft have been delivered to The Queens Flight operating out of RAF Benson. These aircraft are used on domestic and overseas flights by HM The Queen and members of the Royal Family.

Based upon the civilian 100 Series, the aircraft have additional fuel capacity and other modifications, including a specially designed Royal Suite.

Jetstream

    32 Accepted Into Service
     2 "Written Off"
    11 In Squadron Service (Mark T1)
    15 With RNAS Culdrose (Mark T2)
     4 In Various Locations

In Service With:

45 Sqn (R) (6 FTS)   11 x Jetstream T1   RAF Finningley

Crew 2-4; Length 14.37m; Span 15.85m; Height 5.32m; Max Speed 454 km/ph (285 mph); Engines 2 x shp Astazou XV1 D turboprops.
In service with; No 6 Flying Training School

The Jetstream T Mark 1, built by Scottish Aviation, is the military version of the civil light business executive and utility transport aircraft. Jetstream T Mk1 incorporates numerous modifications to meet the requirements of multi-engined pilot training for the RAF, having replaced the much older Varsity in this role. The aircraft is powered by two 940 shp Astazou turboprop engines built by Rolls Royce under an Anglo-French production agreement.

Dominie T1

    20 Accepted Into Service
    18 In Service (Mark T1)
     2 In Various Locations

In Service With:

6 FTS   18 x Dominie T1   RAF Finningley

Crew 2 - 4; Length 14.47m; Span 14.32m; Height 5.03m; Max Speed 805 km/ph (500mph); Engines 2 X Bristol Siddeley Viper 520 turbojets.

The Dominie is the military training version of the well known HS-125 twin-jet executive aircraft and is used by the RAF as a navigation trainer. Powered by 2 x Bristol Siddeley Viper 520 rear-mounted turbojets, each of 3,000 lbs thrust, the Dominie entered service with No 1 Air Navigation School, Stradishall, Suffolk in 1965.

As a navigation aircraft the Dominie is employed at low, medium and high altitudes over a variety of routes. In addition to meeting this primary requirement, the Dominie is also used at the RAF College of Air Warfare by navigation specialists for evaluating or practising new or unusual navigation techniques and for training navigation instructors.

The Dominie provides seating for two pilots (although it is usually flown with only one), two student navigators, a "screen" navigator (whose duty it is to watch over the two students who are putting into practise what they have learnt on the ground) and a supernumerary crew member, or groundcrew member for servicing on overseas flights. The two students sit in rearward facing seats in the rear of the fuselage opposite a students console which is provided with an adequate working surface for charts and instruments etc. Full provision is made for a periscope sextant and a wide variety of electronic navigation aids are included.

The Dominie differs externally from the civil versions in having an extended centre-section, leading edge housing Decca-dolppler aerials and an additional small fin under the tail. In war six Dominie crews, each of four personnel, are assigned to short range maritime patrol duties.

HS 125

    16 Accepted Into Service
    2 In Civilian Use
    1 At DRA Farnborough
    1 at BAe Dunsfold
    12 In Squadron Service

In Service With:

32 Sqn   12 x HS 125 CC1/CC2/CC3 RAF Northolt

700 Series; Span 14.33m; Length 15.46m; Height 5.36m; Weight Empty 5,826 kg; Max Take Off Weight 11,566 kg; Max Speed at 8,500m (28,000 ft) 808 kph (502 mph).

No 32 Squadron operates 12 x HS 125 executive jet aircraft in the high speed/VIP communications role to meet the requirements of Royalty, Ministers of State and senior officers who travel in the UK or overseas.

Four of these aircraft are 400 series introduced in 1971 and capable of carrying up to five passengers. Two aircraft are from the 600 series, introduced in 1973 and six are from the 700 series introduced in 1983. Both of the latter types are capable of carrying up to seven passengers. The smaller 400 Series are easily recognised by the five cabin windows on each side of the fuselage, compared with the six windows in the larger series aircraft.

All marks of the aircraft are powered by twin Garret turbofan engines which enable a cruising speed of between 360 and 420 knots to be maintained at an altitude of up to 41,000 feet over a still air range of 2,000 miles. The aircraft is crewed by two pilots and one steward/stewardess. 32 Squadron has predominantly RAF crews with some Royal Navy pilots included on strength.

Andover

> 37 Accepted Into Service
> (24 x C1; 4 x E3; 3 x E3A; 6 x CC2)
> 2 x C1 "Written Off"
> 5 x C1 "Scrapped"
> 9 x C1 Transferred to RZAF
> 5 x C1/CC2 in Squadron Service
> 7 x E3/E3A in Squadron Service
> 9 x Andover Remain In Various Locations

In Service With:

32 Sqn	5 x Andover C1/CC2*	RAF Northolt
115 Sqn	7 x Andover E3/E3A	RAF RAF Benson**

* 32 Squadron includes 12 x HS125 & 4 x Gazelle.
** The role of 115 Sqn is to be contractorised during October 1993 and the aircraft transferred to Hunting Aviation's base at East Midlands Airport. Once civilian crews have been trained 115 Sqn and the Andover Conversion Flight will disband. Tasking will remain under RAF control.

Crew 2; Passengers - up to 58 or 24 litters and 9 medics; Length (20.42m;Span 31.23m; Height 7.57m; Cruising Speed 451 km/ph (280mph); Service Ceiling 7620m; Range 1456kms with max payload; All Up Operational Weight 23,133kgs; Engines 2 x 17,00Kw Rolls Royce Dart RDa.7 Mk 536-2 turboprops.

The Andover entered service with the RAF in 1966 and has proved to be a reliable short range tactical transport with a useful STOL capability.
The C1 is the basic transport aircraft and the E3 is a version used for flight checking ILS, ground radar and navigation systems. The E3A is another conversion of the aircraft which retains the capability of a short range transport aircraft while being used for the calibration of certain radar/navigation systems.

The CC2 is a development of the commercial Hawker Siddeley 748 short-range airliner, which it closely resembles. It differs from the C1, E3 and E3A in having a shorter fuselage and a lack of "upswept" rear loading tail. The CC2 is used for VIP and communications flying at home and overseas.

Chipmunk T Mark 10

Approximately 60 Aircraft in Service

Crew 2; Length 7.8m; Span 10.3m; Height 2.13m; Max Speed 222 km/ph (138mph); Engine 1 x 1DH Gipsy Major 8 Piston Engine.

The world famous Chipmunk is currently used to give air experience flights to Air Cadets. Initially taken into service with University Air Sqns in 1950 where they were later replaced by the Bulldog we are sure that the Chipmunk will remain in RAF service for some considerable time to come. The aircraft is flown by 12 of the 13 Air Experience Flights.

Bulldog T Mark 1

132 Accepted Into Service
12 Written Off
82 In Service (UAS & Gatow Flight)
38 In Various Locations (FTS etc)

Crew 2; Length 7m; Span 10m; Height 2.28m; Max Speed 241 km/ph (150mph);
Engine 1 x Avco Lycoming IO-360-A1B6 piston engine.

The Bulldog replaced the Chipmunk as the standard RAF basic trainer. The
aircraft is to be found with the University Air Squadrons, the Elementary Flying
Training School, the Central Flying School and is used to provide basic flying
training for helicopter pilots. An RAF order for 132 Bulldogs was placed in 1972
and deliveries commenced in 1973. The RAF model has been structurally
strengthened to increase its fully aerobatic weight and a wider range of instruments
and avionics is fitted. It is powered by a 200 hp Lycoming engine.

Jet Provost

377 JP-T3/T3A/T4/T5/T5A/T5B Accepted into Service
64 "Written Off"
25-30 Remain in Service (Mid 1993)

Note: The locations/final destinations of the other 283 aircraft are too numerous to
list.

(Crew 2; Height 3.34m; Length 10.27m; Span 11.23m; Max Speed 525 km/ph
(409mph); Range 233 kms; Engines 1 x Armstrong Siddeley Viper turbojet.

The Jet Provost was the standard basic jet trainer of the RAF, being an extremely
docile aircraft, yet with a reasonable aerobatic performance. The student pilots
received instruction on the Jet Provost throughout the entire period of their
light-jet training, before progressing to the more advanced Hawk.

The "JP" was taken into service by the RAF in 1955 with the T Mark 1 at No 2
Flying Training School, and the first RAF student to be trained entirely on jet
aircraft, with no previous flying experience flew solo after 8 hours and 20 minutes

instruction. This mark was subsequently upgraded to the T Mark 3. In addition, the RAF also has T Mark 4's with an improved engine and T Mark 5 and 5A&B with further engine improvements and better navigational equipment. We believe that all of the remaining Jet Provost in RAF service were withdrawn during late 1993 and their role assumed by the Tucano.

Tucano

> 130 Accepted Into Service (Early 1994)
>   1 "Written Off"
> 129 Tucano Available

In Service With:

> Central Flying School - RAF Scampton
> 1 FTS - RAF Linton-on-Ouse
> 3 FTS - RAF Cranwell
> 6 FTS - RAF Finningley

Crew 2; Length 9.86m; Height 3.40m; Span 11.14m; Max Speed 458 km/ph (254mph); Service Ceiling 8750m; Range 1916kms; Engine 1100shp Garrett 8TPE-331 turboprop.

Originally designed by the Brazilian aerospace company Embracer, the Tucano was selected in 1985 to replace the Jet Provost as the RAF's basic trainer. The development and production contract was awarded to Shorts of Belfast, who have incorporated a number of modifications to meet the RAF's specifications.

The first aircraft was delivered in June 1988, although two aircraft had been at Boscombe Down undergoing flight trials since late 1987. Student training on the aircraft started at RAF Church Fenton in December 1989.

The RAF version of the Tucano, designated the Tucano T1, has been modified in many ways from the basic Embracer 312. A Garrett TOE 331 engine which develops 1,100 shp, is fitted in place of the original PT6 and represents a 50% power increase. Fatigue life has been extended from 8,000 to 12,000 hours by fitting strengthened wings and landing gear, a ventral air brake has been added, plus a new canopy which is bird strike resistant up to 270 knots.

The Tucano heralds a new concept of flying training within the RAF. The tandem seating, in Martin Baker ejector seats, allows a smaller aerodynamic frontal area than the Jet Provost, leading to lower power requirements and greater fuel efficiency. Visibility from the cockpit is also improved and the student is better prepared to progress to the Hawk advanced trainer. The turbo-engine is both flexible and economic, helping the Tucano to out-perform the Jet Provost in every area except maximum straight-and-level speed. For example, the Tucano time to 15,000 feet is half of that required by the Jet Provost.

The Tucano has been manufactured around the concept of reliability and maintainability to provide a cost-effective trainer and fulfil the requirements of the RAF through the 1990s and beyond.

Skyship 600

Trials are taking place with a Skyship 600 (airship) to identify a variety of possible future RAF roles. The Skyship 600 was supplied by Westinghouse Surveillance Systems Ltd and has an underslung gondola capable of carrying 13 passengers in addition to the pilot. The length of the airship is 59 metres and the range (without auxiliary tanks) is 633 miles (1,019 kms) at 46 mph. The top speed is about 67 mph.

CHAPTER 6 - HELICOPTERS

Chinook

41 Accepted Into Service
3 Lost to Enemy Action (Falklands)
6 "Written Off"
32 Remain In Service

In Service With:

7 Sqn	18 x Chinook HC1/ 1 x Gazelle	RAF Odiham
18 Sqn	5 x Chinook HC1/ 5 x Puma	RAF Laarbruch
27 Sqn (R) (OCU)	4 x Chinook HC1/ 5 x Puma	RAF Odiham
78 Sqn	Chinook HC1	RAF MPA (Falklands)

Crew 3; Fuselage Length 15.54m; Width 3.78m; Height 5.68m; Weight (empty) 10,814kgs; Internal Payload 8,164kgs; Rotor Diameter 18.29m; Cruising Speed 270 km/ph (158mph); Service Ceiling 4,270m; Mission Radius(with internal and external load of 20,000kgs including fuel and crew) 55kms; Rear Loading Ramp Heigh 1.98m; Rear Loading Ramp Width 2.31m; Engines 2 x Avco Lycoming T55-L11E turboshafts.

The Chinook HC1 is a tandem-rotored, twin-engined medium lift helicopter. It has a crew of four (pilot, navigator and 2 x crewmen) and is capable of carrying 45 fully equipped troops or a variety of heavy loads up to approximately 10 tons. The first Chinooks entered service with the RAF in 1982.

The triple hook system allows greater flexibility in load carrying and enables some loads to be carried faster and with greater stability. In the ferry configuration with internally mounted fuel tanks, the Chinook's range is over 1,600 kma (1,000 miles). In the medical evacuation role the aircraft can carry 24 x stretchers.

Chinook aircraft are currently being upgraded to the HC2 standard. The first of the 32 aircraft being upgraded was delivered to the RAF in the Spring of 1993, with the remaining aircraft due to be modified by the end of 1995. The HC2 upgrade, for which a total of 145 million pounds has been allocated (53 million during 1993/94), allows for the aircraft to be modified to the US CH-47D standard with some extra enhancements. These enhancements include fitting infra-red jammers, missile approach warning indicators, chaff and flare dispensers, a long range fuel system and machine gun mountings.

This is a rugged and reliable aircraft. During the Falklands War reports suggest that, at one stage 80 fully equipped troops were carried in one lift and, during a Gulf War mission a single Chinook carried 110 Iraqui POWs. The Chinook mid-life update will significantly enhance the RAF's ability to support the land forces during the next 25 years. Since 1 April 1990 the RAF Chinook fleet has flown some 44,200 hours during which time the operating costs (personnel, fuel and maintenance) have been £232 million, a figure results in a cost of £5,248 per flying hour. On average 18 of the 32 aircraft have been available for front-line service at any one time. This figure reflects the need for planned maintenance and servicing.

Puma

    49 Accepted Into Service
     5 "Written Off"
    37 In Squadron/OCU Service
     7 In Various Locations

In Service With:

18 Sqn	5 x Puma HC1/ 5 x Chinook HC1	RAF Laarbruch
33 Sqn	12 x Puma HC1	RAF Odiham
230 Sqn	15 x Puma HC1	RAF Aldergrove
OCU	5 x Puma HC1/ 4 x Chinook HC1	RAF Odiham

Crew 2 or 3; Fuselage Length 14.06m; Width 3.50m; Height 4.38m; Weight (empty) 3,615kg; Maximum Take Off Weight 7,400kgs; Cruising Speed 258 km/ph (192mph); Service Ceiling 4,800m; Range 550kms; 2 x Turbomecca Turmo 111C4 turbines.

The "package deal" between the UK and France on helicopter collaboration dates back to February 1967 when Ministers of the two countries signed a Memorandum of Understanding (MOU). The programme covered the development of three helicopter types - the Puma, Gazelle and Lynx. The main contractors engaged on the programme were Westland and SNIAS for the airframe, and Rolls Royce and Turbomeca for the engines.

Development of the Puma was already well advanced in France when collaboration began. However, the flight control system has been developed jointly by the two countries, and a great deal of work done by Westland to adapt the helicopter for the particular operational requirements of the RAF. Production of the aircraft was shared between the two countries, the UK making about 20% by value of the airframe, slightly less for the engine as well as assembling the aircraft procured for the RAF. Deliveries of the RAF Pumas started in 1971.

The Puma is powered by 2 x Turbomeca Turmo 111C4 engines mounted side by side above the main cabin. Capable of many operational roles Puma can carry 16 fully equipped troops, or 20 at light scales. In the casualty evacuation role (CASEVAC), 6 stretchers and 6 sitting cases can be carried. Underslung loads of up to 3,200kgs can be transported over short distances and an infantry battalion can be moved using 34 Puma lifts.

Wessex

73 HC2 Accepted Into Service
7 HC2 "Written Off"
54 HC2 In Squadron/FTS Service
12 HC2 In Various Locations

22 Sqn*	11 x Wessex HC2	RAF Chivenor
28 Sqn	8 x Wessex HC2	RAF Sek Kong
60 Sqn	9 x Wessex HC2	RAF Benson
72 Sqn	15 x Wessex HC2	RAF Aldergrove
2 FTS	11 x Wessex HC2	RAF Shawbury
84 Sqn	5 x Wessex HC5C	RAF Akrotiri
Queens Flight	2 x Wessex HCC4	RAF Benson

* 22 Sqn has detachments at Chivenor and Valley.

Crew 1-3; Passengers 16 in main cabin; Length 17.04m; Main Rotor Diameter 17.07m; Height 4.93m; Cabin Door Size 1.22m x 1.22m; Operating Weight 3,767kg; Payload 1,117kg; Max Speed 212km/ph (138mph); Max Range 770kms; Engines 2 X Rolls Royce Bristol Gnome 110/111 turboshafts.

The Wessex HC2 was the first twin-engined, single rotor helicopter to enter service with the RAF and the first production models were delivered in 1962. Since that time, the Wessex has served worldwide and proved to be a rugged, reliable aircraft that can be trusted to perform well in the worst conditions.

In the tactical transport role, the HC Mark 2 can carry 16 troops, or eight stretchers or an underslung load of 1,630kgs. The two other marks in service, are the HC5C which is used for Search and Rescue (SAR) and the HCC Mark 4, an aircraft that is used for VIP transport.

By the beginning of 1996, the Wessex HC2 will be withdrawn from the SAR role and replaced by the Sea King.

Sea King HAR3

19 Sea King HAR3 In RAF Service
6 Sea King HAR3 On Order (Deliveries Complete by 1996)
17 Sea King HAR3 In Squadron Service
2 Sea King HAR3 In Various Locations

In Service With:

202 Sqn*	15 x Sea King HAR3	RAF Boulmer
Falklands SAR	2 x Sea King HAR3	RAF MPA

* 202 Sqn has detachments at Leconfield, Boulmer, Lossiemouth and Wattisham.

Crew 1-3; Length 17.01m; Height 4.72m; Rotor Diameter 18.9m; Weight (empty) 6201kg; Cruising Speed 208 km/ph (129mph); Range 1230kms; Engine 2 x Rolls Royce Gnome H1400.1 turboshafts.

The Westland Sea King HAR3 Search and Rescue helicopter entered RAF service in 1978. The aircraft is powered by two Rolls Royce Gnome gas turbine engines, each rated at 1,660 shaft horse power and is fitted with advanced all-weather search and navigation equipment, as well as autopilot and onboard computer to assist positioning and hovering at night, or in bad weather. In addition to four crew members the HAR3 can carry up to six stretchers, or 18 survivors. Under normal conditions expect the HAR3 to have an operational radius of approximately 448 kms (280 miles).

The Sea King HAR3 will replace the Wessex HC2 in the SAR role by 1996. A recent MOD report concluded that a total of 25 Sea Kings were required to ensure that SAR duties were carried out effectively and an announcement was made in mid 1992 of an order for 6 more HAR3, to bring the total up to the required 25. Of this 25 aircraft, 12 will be required for SAR duties in the UK, 2 in the Falkland Islands, 4 will be necessary for conversion training and the remaining 7 will form an engineering and operational pool.

SAR Operations are examined in more detail in the Chapter on RAF Roles.

Gazelle

28 x Gazelle HT3 In RAF Service

In Service With:

No 32 Sqn	4 x Gazelle HT3/5 x Andover/12 x HS125	RAF Northolt
No 2 FTS	24 x Gazelle HT3	RAF Shawbury

Crew 2; Fuselage Length 9.53m; Height 3.15m; Main Rotor Diameter 10.5m; Max Speed 264 km/ph (164mph); Service Ceiling 5000m; Range 670kms; Engine 1 x Turbomeca Astazou 3C turboshaft.

The Anglo-French Gazelle light helicopter is used by the RAF in the basic helicopter training and communications roles. The HT Mark 3 is the training version and the majority are based at RAF Shawbury, with four aircraft in No 32 Sqn. World wide over 1,000 Gazelles are in service.

Sidewinder AIM-9L

Diameter 0.127m: Span 0.63m: Length 2.85m: Total Weight 85.3kgs: Warhead Weight 10.2kg: Propulsion Solid fuel rocket: Speed Mach 2.5: Range 17.7kms.

The Sidewinder missile which is carried by all of the RAF's air defence aircraft, is an infra-red weapon which homes onto the heat emitted by a hostile aircraft's engines. Sidewinder can operate independently of the aircraft's radar, and provides the air defence aircraft with an alternative method of attacking targets at shorter ranges. Sidewinder has an excellent dogfight capability.

Sparrow AIM-7F

Length 3.66m: Diameter 0.203m: Span 1.02m: Weight 228kgs: Warhead Weight 39kgs: Speed: Mach 4: Range 70kms: Propulsion dual thrust solid fuel rocket.

The Sparrow missile was carried as an alternative to the Sky Flash by the Phantom Air Defence Fighter. It is radar guided and has an all-weather all-aspect capability against supersonic and slower flying aircraft, flying at very high altitude or down to sea level. Sparrow is believed to have been withdrawn from service at the same time as the Phantom.

Sky Flash

As for Sparrow except: Marconi monopulse semi - active radar homing system: Warhead 30kg: Total Weight 192.3kg: Range 50kms.

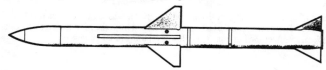

Sky Flash is an advanced radar guided air-to-air missile based on the Sparrow which was taken into service in 1977, but with improved guidance and fusing systems. Designed to operate in severe electronic counter-measure conditions, it has an all weather high/low altitude attack capability. Sky Flash is in service on F3 air defence variant of the Tornado. It is currently the RAF's major air defence weapon.

Harpoon

Length 3.84m: Diameter 0.343m: Span 1.20m: Total Weight 526kg: Warhead Weight 225kg: Speed Mach 0.85: Propulsion 1 x Aerojet solid-fuel booster rocket delivering 6600kg of thrust and 1 x Teledyne sustainer turbojet delivering 308kg of thrust: Range 110kms.

Harpoon, manufactured by McDonnel Douglas of the USA, is an extremely powerful anti-shipping missile, that was first fitted to RAF Nimrods during the Falklands War. The missile can be launched from the Nimrod bomb bay, and in-flight corrections can be made by the missile's computer using information gathered by a variety of on-board sensors. The missile is difficult to detect by the target because its final track is very low and very close to the surface of the sea. The warhead is extremely powerful and a hit from Harpoon is almost certain to result in the destruction or disablement of a major surface vessel.

Although this weapon does not appear to be listed in the current RAF inventory, we believe that stocks remain in the depots. It is believed that Nimrod aircraft have been armed with Harpoon in the past.

Sea Eagle

Length 4.14m: Diameter 0.40m: Span 1.20m: Total Weight 590kg: Warhead Weight (not yet revealed) believed to be 200kg+: Speed Mach 0.9+: Range 50-100kms depending on launch altitude: Propulsion 1 x Microturbo TRI -l-60-1 turbojet delivering 367kg of thrust.

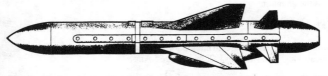

The Sea Eagle, a long range anti-ship guided missile, is used by the Tornado GR1 and Nimrod in the maritime attack role. Developed from the Martel, Sea Eagle can attack targets over the horizon at very low level using radar guidance and an on-board microprocessor which stores the target's last known position and speed. Powered by a small air-breathing-turbojet, the missile skims the waves at just under the speed of sound and picks up the target with its very advanced active radar seeker.

ALARM

Length 4.24m: Diameter 0.22m: Span 0.72m: Total Weight 175kg: Propellant 1 x Royal Ordnance Nuthatch solid fuel two stage rocket: Range and speed not yet revealed, however these figures are probably comparable with those of HARM which has a speed of Mach 3+ and a range of 75kms+.

ALARM stands for Air Launched Anti-Radiation Missile and this type has recently been introduced into RAF Service. The missile is launched at low level near the suspected site of an enemy radar and after launch rapidly climbs to about 12,000m. At this height, a small parachute opens and the missile descends earthwards while the on-board radar searches the broad band for emissions from enemy radar. Once a target has been identified, the motor is re-ignited and the missile makes a supersonic dive onto the target.

The total RAF buy in the first manufacturing run was believed to be some 750 missiles.

ASRAAM

Length 2.7 metres.

The ASRAAM (Advanced Short Range Air to Air Missile) fire-and-forget missile, is an air combat weapon that is highly manoeuvrable and requires minimal pilot input. The missile has an advanced high sensitivity infra-red seeker, which can lock onto the target before launch or in flight, and results in an extremely high kill probability. ASRAAM is also highly resistant to electronic countermeasures. We believe that the current planned RAF in service date (ISD) for the missile is 1998.

AMRAAM

Length 3.6 metres; weight 340 lbs; cruising speed Mach 4; range approx 30 miles.

AMRAAM (Advanced medium range air-to-air missile)is an air fighting weapon that matches the fire-and-forget capability of the ASRAAM, but with greater range. There is increased immunity over electronic countermeasures and a low-smoke, high impulse rocket motor to reduce the probability of an enemy sighting the missile.

Present plans for the RAF are unclear. However, AMRAAM will be in service with the Fleet Air Arm from 1995 and the initial purchase is believed to be about 210 missiles.

Martel

Length 3.87m; Span 1.2m; Total Weight 550kgs; Warhead Weight 150kgs; Propulsion 1 x Solid Fuel booster rocket and one solid fuel sustainer rocket; Speed Mach 2; Range 60kms (from a high altitude launch) to 30kms (from a low altitude launch).

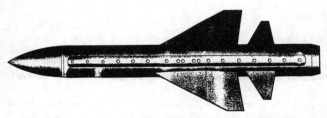

The Martel missile forms part of the under-wing armament of the Buccaneer low-level maritime attack aircraft. Featuring stand off ability, the missile's guidance system is of the television relay type or alternatively it can home on to enemy radar transmissions. Martel will probably be withdrawn from service when the last Buccaneer squadron disbands on 1 April 1994.

BL 755 Cluster Bomb

Length 2.45m: Diameter .41m: Weight 277kg: Payload 147 bomblets.

The BL 755 is a system which was designed to cope with some of the very large area targets that might be encountered on the Central front, especially large armoured formations of Regimental strength (90+ tanks) or more. The weapon can be carried by Tornado GR1, Harrier, and Jaguar and consists of a large container which is divided into seven compartments. Each of these compartments contains 21 bomblets making a total of 147 bomblets in all.

After the bomb has been released from the aircraft, the 147 bomblets are ejected and fall to the ground covering a wide area. As each individual bomblet hits a target, a HEAT charge is detonated which can fire a large slug of molten metal through up to 250mm of armour. In addition, the casing of the bomblet disintegrates and hundreds of fragments of shrapnel are dispersed over a wide area, with resultant damage to personnel and soft skinned vehicles.

The BL 755 can be released at very low altitude and this is essential if pilots are to survive in the high density SAM conditions that could apply over the Central Front. Aircraft will only have the chance to make one pass over the target before the defences are alerted, and for a pilot to make a second pass to ensure accuracy would be suicidal

JP 233 Airfield Attack System

Designed for use by the Tornado GR1, the JP 233 has only recently entered RAF service. A Tornado will carry two JP 233 systems and each system is comprised of a dispenser which releases 30 cratering sub-munitions and 215 area denial sub-munitions (mines) over a wide area. The cratering sub-munitions penetrate the runway and explode leaving large holes which render its use by aircraft impossible. The area denial sub-munitions rest on the surface in the vicinity of the craters and make repair work very dangerous until cleared by specialist teams.

JP 233 has a variety of uses against a whole range of targets besides airfields.

WE 177 Free Fall Bomb

The United Kingdom's sub strategic nuclear capability is currently provided by the WE 177 bomb carried on the Tornado dual-capable aircraft. There is a current programme to extend the life of the WE 177 free fall bomb, to provide an effective capability into the first decade of the next century.
During 1993/94 some £20 million has been allocated for non warhead costs, security and operating the WE177.

THAAD

Recent fears of nuclear proliferation, and the problems of nuclear capable delivery systems such as the former Soviet Scud missile being used by nations who hitherto have not been able to mount a credible threat to the UK, have forced the MOD to look at the options offered by adopting a high level missile defence.

We believe that the UK MOD is now looking at a Theatre High-Altitude Area Defence (THAAD) system for defending the UK against incoming missiles. The MOD appears to be interested in creating a layered anti-missile defence, capable of multiple attempts at hitting targets at ranges of over 100 miles at at heights of over 100,000 feet, to shorter range systems such as the US Patriot that could hit targets at much closer range.

During late 1993, officials from the US Lockheed Corporation briefed UK MOD staff on the capabilities of THAAD, and in November 1993, more than 60 companies attended a presentation regarding work on such a system. However, we believe that the UK can only proceed in such an expensive programme as a partner in a European collaborative project, and there are some reports that preliminary talks have taken place to explore options.

A layered system based upon low, medium and high level missiles, employing satellite and early warning aircraft detectors would have a very high percentage chance of success against everything except a saturation attack by large numbers of missiles. However, the defence budgets of the nations that really count in the European procurement scene (France, Germany and the UK) appear to be fully committed until at least 2005. An expensive THAAD system costing many billions of pounds is almost certainly not going to appear in the short term.

In February 1994, the UK Secretary of State for Defence announced that a £3.5 million study into ballistic missile defences would take place.

TASM

Due to the reduction in the level of the threat following the demise of the Warsaw Pact, plans for the development of an air to surface stand-off nuclear weapon (TASM) have been shelved. However, TASM is a nuclear system and the Secretary of State for Defence clearly stated on 18 Oct 93, that with regards to conventional stand off weapons, "a quite separate system will continue in the RAF's programme".

MSAM

In February 1991, it was announced that the Bloodhound (in service since 1958) medium range surface to air missile (MSAM) would be retired. At the time of the Bloodhound retirement it was believed that a successor MSAM would be introduced into service by the mid 1990s. The Defence Committee of the House of Commons expressed its dismay that "that a significant part of our air defences should have become obsolete without a replacement having been procured" and called upon the MOD to "press ahead urgently with its plans to procure a medium range surface to air missile".

In 1992, an MOD spokesman announced "we have concluded that there is insufficient requirement in the near-term for a MSAM. We are now reconsidering the nature and timing of any longer term requirement for such a capability". However, in July 1992 the Secretary of State for Defence further stated "There is likely to be a longer term need and we are continuing our studies into these options".

CHAPTER 8 - TRAINING

Following selection, potential officers attend the Initial Officer Training Course at the Royal Air Force College Cranwell. The course lasts for eighteen weeks and at the end of the course students are commissioned as Pilot Officers (some University Graduates may already have been commissioned and on completing the course at Cranwell their commissions are confirmed). Following the course at the Department of Initial Officer Training, officers move to a variety of training schools to achieve some competence in the specialisation of their choice.

Officer Branches In The Royal Air Force

Branch	Max Age On Entry
Pilot	24 (26 if in the RAF)
Navigator	26
Air Traffic Control	30
Fighter Control	30
Intelligence	30
Engineer	39
Supply	30 (Exceptionally 39)
Administration	30
Education	30 (Exceptionally 39)
Catering	39
Physical Education	27 (Exceptionally 30)
RAF Regiment	26
RAF Police	30 (Exceptionally 39)
Medical	39
Medical Secretarial	30 (Exceptionally 39)
Dental	33
PMRAFNS	34 (Exceptionally +34)
Chaplain	34 (Exceptionally +34)
Legal	32 (Exceptionally +32)

Flying Training

After Initial Officer Training, potential pilots without previous flying experience go to the Elementary Flying Training Sqn at RAF Topcliffe for up to 60+ hours flying on Bulldog/civilian aircraft. Those assessed as suitable proceed to basic flying training, which is carried out at No 1 FTS RAF Linton-on-Ouse or No 3 FTS RAF College Cranwell.

Some entrants will have already had some previous flying experience. University Air Squadrons generally provide up to 100 hours flying on Bulldog aircraft and recipients of RAF Flying Scholarships have 30 hours of flying training on civilian aircraft at RAF expense.

During this basic flying training phase at RAF Linton-on-Ouse or RAF Cranwell, pilots are selected for one of three streams of advanced training. Fast jet pilots for air defence and ground attack squadrons go to No 4 FTS at RAF Valley to fly Hawks; multi-engine aircraft training is carried out at No 6 FTS at RAF Finningley on Jetstreams, and helicopter training using Wessex and Gazelle is carried out at No 2 FTS RAF Shawbury. Each of these types of advanced flying training takes the pilot to "wings" standard.

At No 6 FTS RAF Finningley, all branches of aircrew are trained. In addition to multi-engined training, navigators fly in Dominie, Tucano and Hawk aircraft to gain experience at both low and high level, the flying time spent on particular types determining the student's future role. Air engineers and air electronics operators start flying as acting sergeant aircrew following a six week Airman Aircrew Initial Training Course - a course similar to Initial Officer Training at Cranwell. The airman aircrew train alongside the navigators in Dominies. Air loadmasters also do their basic training at RAF Finningley before joining their squadrons.

RAF Scampton is the home of the Central Flying School (CFS), the oldest flying training establishment in the world. The main functions of the CFS are to train flying instructors for all of the three Services as well as for a number of overseas Services. Additionally, the CFS monitors the standards of flying instruction across the RAF.

RAF Flying Hours

Fast Jet Pilots

EFTS	RAF Topcliffe	60+hours	Bulldog/T-67M
1 FTS	RAF Linton-on-Ouse	146 hours (long course)	Tucano
		130 hours (short course)	Tucano
3 FTS	RAF Cranwell	146 hours (long course)	Tucano
		130 hours (short course)	Tucano
4 FTS	RAF Valley	65 hours (conversion)	Hawk
		35 hours (tactics & wpns)	Hawk

Multi-Engine Pilots

EFTS	RAF Topcliffe	63 hours	Bulldog/civil
1 FTS	RAF Linton-on-Ouse	140 hours (long course)	Tucano
		123 hours (short course)	Tucano
3 FTS	RAF Cranwell	140 hours (long course)	Tucano
		123 hours (short course)	Tucano
6 FTS	RAF Finningley	50 hours	Jetstream

Helicopter Pilots

EFTS	RAF Topcliffe	63 hours	Bulldog/civil
1 FTS	RAF Linton-on-Ouse	63.5 hours (long course)	Tucano
		49.5 hours (short course)	Tucano
3 FTS	RAF Cranwell	63.5 hours (long course)	Tucano
		49.5 hours (short course)	Tucano
2 FTS	RAF Shawbury	80 hours	Gazelle
		65 hours	Wessex

Having completed advanced training, pilots will then be posted to the relevant OCU/Training Units as follows:

Tornado OCU (TWCU)	RAF Lossiemouth	(15 Reserve Sqn)
Tornado F3 OCU	RAF Coningsby	(56 Reserve Sqn)
Jaguar OCU	RAF Lossiemouth	(16 Reserve Sqn)
Harrier OCU	RAF Wittering	(20 Reserve Sqn)
Nimrod OCU	RAF Kinloss	(42 Reserve Sqn)
Helicopter OCU	RAF Odiham	(27 Reserve Sqn)
Hercules OCU	RAF Lyneham	(57 Reserve Sqn)
VC-10/Tristar OCU	RAF Brize Norton	(55 Reserve Sqn)
SARTU (1)	RAF Valley(tf)	
SKTU (2)	RAF St Mawgan	
TTTE (3)	RAF Cottesmore	
Andover Trg Flt	RAF Benson	
Sentry Trg Sqn	RAF Waddington	
Canberra Trg Flight	RAF Wyton	

Notes: (1) Search & Rescue Training Unit (2) Sea King Training Unit (3) TTTE - Trinational Tornado Training Establishment.

Pilot Requirements

The annual continuation training requirement for simulator training for Tornado GR1/1A and Harrier GR5/GR7 pilots is 20 hours. To retain combat ready status on Tornado GR1/1A and Harrier GR5/GR7, pilots must fly a minimum of 180 hours per year (15 hours monthly). Tornado GR1 pilots must complete a minimum of eight hours automatic terrain following radar (TFR) flying per year.

Operational Low Flying (OLF)

All combat ready RAF fast jet aircrew except Tornado F3 aircrew are required to be current in operational low flying down to 100 feet. These aircrew may be required to fly a small number of continuation training sorties before deploying to operational theatres overseas.

Air crews qualified to conduct operational low flying (OLF) maintain currency by flying a minimum of four overland OLF sorties, with a maximum of six in any six month period and a maximum of ten in any 12 month period. OLF currency is valid for six months. Lapsed currency may be regained by Tornado IDS crews flying 5 OLF sorties, and by Jaguar and Harrier pilots flying 4 OLF sorties. OLF sorties conducted over the sea do not contribute to the maintenance of OLF currency.

Low Flying Sorties

During the month of November 1993 low flying sorties over the UK were as follows:

Buccaneer	54	F-111	5
Harrier	471	F-15	288
Hawk	486	**Total**	**5669**
Jaguar	390		
Tornado	1280		
Tucano	380		
Other (incl helicopters)	2315		

On average during 1993, some 9,000 low flying sorties were carried out each month. Of this figure, some 200 are usually C-130 Hercules sorties and just over 3400 are helicopter sorties. The remaining 5,400 monthly sorties are fast jet.

MSD

There are demanding standards required for crews of other aircraft types. For example, the crews of C-130 Hercules are trained to fly at a minimum separation distance (MSD) from other aircraft in a formation - eg whilst dropping parachutists. Following at least six months service on operational Hercules Sqns, crews are trained to fly aircraft at 500ft (150 metres) MSD; this aspect of training requires four sorties totalling 12 flying hours. Subsequently, after six months service on tactical support squadrons, crews are selected for training to fly at 250 ft (75 metres) MSD; this training consists of 20 sorties totalling 41 flying hours. Approximately six months after qualifying to fly at 250 ft MSD crews undertake a further training course of 5 sorties totalling 12 flying hours. Of these crews, a very small number are permitted to fly at under 250 ft MSD.

Ex Red Flag

In order to improve standards and operation readiness, RAF aircrews take part in exercises world wide, often in concert with other NATO air forces. For example the RAF has been a regular participant in the Red Flag exercises since the mid 1970s. Red Flag is a combat exercise usually lasting for about six weeks and is held at the USAF Nellis Air Force Base (Nevada).

Nellis AFB has a number of F-16C Fighting Falcons formed into the Adversary Tactics Division, with pilots trained in the tactics of potential enemy air forces. During the April - May 1992 Red Flag exercise RAF involvement included:

> 8 x Tornado GR1(tf)
> 6 x Tornado F3(t)
> 1 x AEW1 Sentry(tf)
> 1 x VC-10 Tanker(tf)
> 1 x C-130 Hercules(tf)

During the exercise, the GR1 practised ground attack, penetrating simulated ground and air defences, with F3's as fighter escorts attempting to keep the F-16C aggressors away from the attacking GR1s. Results from the exercise are fed into a massive computer system "Red Flag Measurement and Debriefing System (RFMDS). Using the RFMDS the exercise staff can debrief crews on results and tactics.

Female Pilots

As of 19 Oct 93, there 8 x female pilots with a further 17 trained navigators. A further 21 pilots and 6 navigators were undergoing training. Of the eight trained pilots, two have qualified as fast-jet pilots and will be undertaking Tornado training. The remaining six are serving either as flying instructors, as search and rescue helicopter pilots, or as co-pilots in Hercules transport aircraft.

Ranges and Types Air Weaponry Used on UK Air-to-Ground Ranges

Ballykelly	-	Guns
Castle Martin	-	Guided Weapons (GW) and guns
Cowden	-	Practice and inert bombs
Donna Nook	-	Guns, rockets, practice & inert bombs
Garvie Island	-	Bombs & GW

Holbeach	-	Guns, rockets, practice & inert bombs, GW
Larkhill	-	HE bombs, practice bombs, guns, rockets & GW
Lilstock	-	Practice bombs
Lulworth	-	GW & guns
Otterburn	-	GW & guns
Pembrey Sands	-	Guns & practice bombs
Rosehearty	-	Rockets, practice & inert bombs
Salisbury Plain	-	GW & guns
Shoeburyness	-	GW
Tain	-	Guns, rockets, practice & inert bombs
Wainfleet	-	Guns, rockets, practice & inert bombs
West Freugh	-	HE bombs, practice & cluster bombs, guns & rockets
Wiley Sike	-	Practice bombs

Ground Training

The schools for training engineering and supply officers are at the RAF College Cranwell. Air Traffic Control training is carried out at RAF Shawbury, secretarial training at RAF Halton and catering at Aldershot. Education officers, most of whom will have university degrees, go to the RAF School of Education and Training Support at RAF Newton, which is also the current home of the RAF Police School. There are also courses for those officers, such as entrants to the Medical branch, who will have entered the RAF professionally qualified, but who require courses to orientate them in the ways of the service.

To sustain the RAF through the manpower changes of the 1990, it will probably be necessary to train an average intake of 4,000 to 5,000 annually during the second half of the decade. Both airmen and airwomen start with six weeks basic training at the School of Recruit Training at RAF Halton. These non-commissioned personnel may join for training in 70 separate trades.

Following recruit training, non commissioned personnel proceed to specialised training. By far the largest training task is concerned with engineering tradesmen and the schools at RAF Cosford, RAF Locking and RAF St Athan carry out the bulk of this training. At the Airman's Command School at RAF Halton, there are two General Service Training Courses; one for airmen/airwomen provisionally selected for promotion to Corporal and the other for Corporals about to become Sergeants.

The RAF provides about 700 different ground training courses. These can vary from two weeks for qualified typists to learn Service techniques, to technical training courses lasting over 18 months. Many courses are devised specially to meet particular requirements as new equipments enter service.

RAF Airman/Airwomen Trades Requiring Qualifications*

Airframe Mechanic (Tech Stream); Propulsion Mechanic (Tech Stream); Weapons Mechanic (Tech Stream); Aircraft Electrical Mechanic (Tech Stream); Avionics Mechanic (Tech Stream); Synthetic Trainer Mechanic (Tech Stream); Electronic Technician (Air Defence); Electronic Technician (Airfield); Electronic Technician (Telecommunications); General Technician (Electrical); General Technician (Ground Support Equipment); General Technician (Workshops); Mechanical Transport Technician; Chef (Qualified); Steward (Qualified); Communications Systems Analyst (Voice); Communications System Analyst; Air Cartographer; Musician; Laboratory Technician; Physiotherapist (Qualified); Staff Nurse (Qualified); Mental Nurse; Environmental Health Technician; Operating Theatre Technician; Electrophysiological Technician; Pharmacy Technician; Radiographer; Dental Hygienist.

* All of these trades require entry qualifications of between 2- 5 GCSE's or recognised professional qualifications.

RAF Airman/Airwomen Trades Not Requiring Formal Entry Qualifications

Airframe Mechanic; Propulsion Mechanic; Weapons Mechanic; Aircraft Electrical Mechanic; Avionics Mechanic; Synthetic Trainer Mechanic; Electronic Mechanic (Air Defence); Electronic Mechanic (Airfield); Electronic Mechanic (Telecommunications); General Mechanic (Electrical); General Mechanic (Ground Support Equipment); General Mechanic (Workshops); Aerial Erector; Mechanical Transport Mechanic; Mechanical Transport Driver; RAF Police; Kennel Assistant; Supplier; Movements Operator; Clerk Catering; Chef (Unqualified); Steward (Unqualified); RAF Regiment Gunner; Fireman; Assistant Air Traffic Controller; Physical Training Instructor; RAF Administrative; RAF General Duties; Telecommunications Operator; Aerospace Systems Operator; Painter and Finisher; Survival Equipment Fitter; Air Photography Processor 2; Photographer Ground; Photographic Interpreter (Assistant); Personnel Administrator; Data Analyst; Shorthand Typist; Typist; Enrolled Nurse (General); Medical Assistant; Dental Assistant.

Sergeant Aircrew

	Max Entry Age	Minimum Qualifications
Air Engineer	26*	Eng Lang/Maths/Physics
Air Electronics Operator	26	Eng Lang/Maths/Physics
Air Loadmaster	26	Eng Lang plus 2 others

* In exceptional cases entrants for all sergeant aircrew specialisations may be aged up to 31.

Command and Staff Training

The fundamental requirements of an RAF officer are professional competence in his specialist role and executive ability. However, as the officer advances in rank, he or she is expected to cover wider areas of responsibility and command staff training is designed to develop this breadth, RAF PTC is responsible for the four week officers Command School Course at RAF Henlow, which is the first non-professional course after specialist training. It is followed by the individual Staff Studies course, a correspondence course lasting 18 months, which is a prerequisite for further staff training. Squadron Leaders may be selected to attend the Basic Staff Course, which will lead for some to the 10 month Advanced Staff Course for Squadron Leaders and Wing Commanders. All staff training is the responsibility of the RAF Staff College Bracknell, Berkshire.

Air Training Corps

The Air Training Corps (ATC) exists to encourage an interest in aviation and the RAF, for young people from the age of 13, and to provide training for the Services and civilian life, while nurturing a spirit of adventure and promoting leadership qualities.

The Air Officer Commanding Air Cadets (a serving Air Commodore) is also the Commandant of the Air Training Corps and Director of Reserve Forces. He is responsible for some 44,000 cadets in 906 Squadrons & 83 Detached Flights, formed into 40 Wings throughout the country. HQ Air Cadets is located at RAF Newton.

All Air Cadets have the opportunity to gain gliding experience, and some go solo at one of the 28 Volunteer Gliding Schools operating Viking or Vigilant gliders throughout the UK. Air Cadets also fly in the Chipmunk aircraft from one of the 13 Air Experience Flights located at airfields in the UK.
The ATC traces its origins to the British Young Airman's League formed in 1928 and in 1938 prior to the beginning of WWII, the first squadrons of the Air Defence Cadet Corps were formed. The ATC was formed in September 1940 and very quickly became one of the main sources of RAF recruitment.

During the Financial Year 1992-93, the Ministry of Defence's contribution to the costs of the ATC were £17.9 million, or in the words of Viscount Ridley in the House of Lords on 3 Feb 94, "almost exactly the same as the compensation which is likely to be paid to 100 dismissed pregnant WRENs". As does Viscount Ridley, many believe that this is money well spent and the returns are out of all proportion to the outlay. Currently some 23% of airmen and 57% of RAF Officers have cadet experience prior to regular service.

Air Experience Flights (AEF)

1 AEF   Manston

2 AEF	Hurn
3 AEF	Colerne
4 AEF	Exeter Airport
5 AEF	Cambridge
6 AEF	Benson
7 AEF	Newton
8 AEF	Shawbury
9 AEF	Finningley
10 AEF	Woodvale
11 AEF	Leeming
12 AEF	Turnhouse
13 AEF	Aldergrove

Note: An AEF generally has between 4 - 6 Chipmunk T-10 aircraft. The major exception to this rule is 13 AEF which it is believed borrows Bulldog aircraft from Queens UAS as required. As an example, No 12 AEF at Turnhouse is reported to be achieving some 2,000 flying hours per year (4,000 cadet flights) with additional weekend and annual camp flights from Kinloss, Leuchars and Lossiemouth.

Volunteer Gliding Schools (VGS)

611 VGS	Swanton Morley *
612 VGS	Halton
613 VGS	Halton
614 VGS	Weathersfield
615 VGS	Kenley
616 VGS	Henlow
617 VGS	Manston
618 VGS	West Malling
621 VGS	Hullavington
622 VGS	Upavon
624 VGS	Chivenor
625 VGS	Hullavington
626 VGS	Predanack
631 VGS	Sealand
632 VGS	Ternhill
633 VGS	Cosford
634 VGS	St Athan
635 VGS	Samlesbury
636 VGS	Swansea
637 VGS	Little Rissington
642 VGS	Linton-on-Ouse
643 VGS	Scampton
644 VGS	Syerston
645 VGS	Catterick

661 VGS	Kirknewton
662 VGS	Arbroath
663 VGS	Kinloss

Note: * Expect a VGS to have between 4-6 Vigilant or Viking Gliders

* ACCS	(Air Cadets Central Gliding School)	-	Syerston	-	2 x Kestrel TX1
					3 x Valiant TX1
					13 x Vigilant TX1
					12 x Viking TX1

University Air Squadrons (UAS)

University Air Squadrons exist to give undergraduates flying experience and each unit is commanded by a regular RAF officer assisted by some regular staff. Generally speaking, a student can be expected to receive up to 100 hours flying training during time at the UAS.

Aberdeen & St Andrews UAS	Leuchars
Birmingham	Cosford
Bristol	Colerne
Cambridge	Teversham
East Lowlands UAS	Turnhouse
East Midlands UAS	Newton
Glasgow & Strathclyde UAS	Abbotsinch
Liverpool UAS	Woodvale
London UAS	Benson
Manchester UAS	Woodvale
Northumbrian UAS	Leeming
Oxford UAS	Benson
Queens UAS	Aldergrove
Southampton UAS	RNAS Lee-on-Solent
Wales UAS	St Athan
Yorkshire UAS	Finningley

Note: UAS will generally be equipped with 4-5 Bulldog aircraft. The exceptions to this rule are London UAS with 9-10 x Bulldog and Yorkshire UAS with 8-9 x Bulldog.

Sponsorship

Sixth Form Scholarships - Students expecting to pass 5 x GCSE's or equivalent can try for an RAF Scholarship. This provides a grant during the two years of their A-Level course and opens the way to a commission. Candidates go through the full selection procedure at the Officers and Aircrew Selection Centre (RAF Cranwell).

Flying Scholarships - The Flying Scholarship Scheme offers suitably qualified young men and women (between the ages of 16 and 21) 30 hours free instruction (including ten hours solo) at a selected civilian flying club. Applicants must have five appropriate GCSE's or equivalent and must pass the preliminary medical and aptitude tests used for selecting RAF officers and aircrew.

University Cadetships - Candidates who are filling in an UCCA form, or who have already started at a university on a degree course may apply for a University Cadetship. This provides a salary as a commissioned Acting Pilot Officer and pays for all course fees other than board and lodging. On graduation, Cadets enter full-time training as as Pilot Officers.

University Bursaries - University Bursaries may be awarded to those who initially wish to commit themselves to no more than a Short Service Commission (lasting from 3 to 6 years). The RAF provides financial support to supplement the local authority grant and no more is expected of the student than a reasonable level of academic attainment during the degree course. Bursary holders remain civilians during the period of their studies and will be appointed to a commission on graduation. The minimum length of Short Service Commission depends upon the branch into which the Bursar will later be commissioned.

CHAPTER 9 - RAF SUPPORT ORGANISATIONS

Search & Rescue (SAR)

The RAF's Search and Rescue (SAR) service provides all year round emergency for those in peril at sea and on land. Although primarily intended as a military emergency service, the majority of SAR work involves civilian incidents. SAR organisation consists of three units; the Rescue Co-ordination Centre (RCCs), the flying units and the mountain rescue teams.

Two RCCs, one at Pitreavie Castle, Dunfermline and the other at RAF St Mawgan are responsible for co-ordinating calls for assistance and the subsequent rescue operations.

The flying units consist of four aircraft types. The Nimrod maritime patrol aircraft can be used to search for survivors and give guidance to rescue craft and helicopters at the scene of the incident. It can also drop survival equipment and life rafts if needed. The Sentry AEW aircraft could be used to locate radar distress beacons, but would be most useful providing communication links and any control required at the scene of an incident.

Six helicopter flights are evenly distributed around the coast of the United Kingdom to provide maritime and land rescue cover 24 hours a day -365 days a year. These units are either currently equipped with, or converting to Sea King Mk3 helicopters. The Sea King is one of the most capable search and rescue helicopters in current service. It has an automatic flight control system enabling transition from forward flight to an automatic doppler hover. Used in conjunction with its homing aids and radar, this enables a full instrument recovery to be made, giving it a true all weather capability. The aircraft has a radius of action of 280 nautical miles and the carrying capacity for 18 survivors. The crew of four consists of two pilots, a radar/winch operator and a winchman.

In May 1990, the RAF completed one of the World's longest rescue missions when a Sea King from RAF Brawdy in South Wales, recovered an injured crewman from the yacht Liverpool Enterprise which was on the final leg of the Whitbread "Round the World" yacht race. The rescue took place 610 miles West South West of Lands End and involved a 13-hour flight, which included refuelling stops in Southern Ireland and on RFA Argus. The eventual rescue lift was carried out successfully at night and the casualty taken to Cork hospital.

During October 1992 the UK MOD announced substantial changes to the UK SAR organisation, with the future helicopter fleet to be composed entirely of Sea Kings, the older Wessex withdrawn from service and the bases "rationalised". During 1992 the SAR helicopter fleet consisted of 19 x Sea King Mk3 and 14 x Wessex Mk2 stationed at nine bases. No 22 Sqn operated Wessex at Coltishall, Valley, Leuchars and Chivenor and 202 Sqn operated Sea Kings at Leconfield, Boulmer, Lossiemouth, Manston and Brawdy. Two Sea Kings were based in the Falklands and other aircraft used for training and engineering.

As a result of a study into possible wartime requirements, the MOD concluded that a force of 25 x Sea Kings were necessary and the purchase of six more aircraft was announced in the House of Commons during February 1992 - the in service date (ISD) for these aircraft is 1996. Of this total of 25 aircraft, 12 will be on permanent standby for SAR duties in the UK area, 2 will continue to provide SAR cover in the Falklands, 4 will provide conversion training and the remaining 7 will provide an operational and engineering reserve. Under the new organisation 2 x Sea King will be based at each of the following locations:-

Leconfield	202 Sqn	
Lossiemouth	202 Sqn	
Boulmer	202 Sqn	
Chivenor	22 Sqn	
Valley	22 Sqn	(Sea King from 1996)
Wattisham	202 Sqn	

The Sea King Training Unit (SKTU) will be based at RAF St Mawgan and the RAF will continue to operate SAR in Northern Ireland with a helicopter based at RAF Aldergrove. In addition to the RAF SAR units, both the Royal Navy and HM Coastguard operate SAR units to ensure complete UK coverage as follows:

Royal Navy	Prestwick	Sea King
Royal Navy	Culdrose	Sea King
Royal Navy	Portland	Sea King
HM Coastguard	Lee-on-Solent	S61
HM Coastguard	Stornoway	S61
HM Coastguard	Sumburg (Shetlands)(t)S61	

SAR Call Outs 1992

RCC Edinburgh

Boulmer	134
Coltishall (withdraws mid 1994)	97
Lossiemouth	241
Leuchars (withdrawn 1993)	131
Valley	187
Leconfield	159
Prestwick	168
Sumburg	16

Stornoway	69
Others	15
RCC Plymouth	
Brawdy (withdraws mid 1994)	154
Chivenor	174
Manston (Wattisham mid 1994)	159
Culdrose	233
Portland	138
Coltishall (withdraws mid-1994)	9
Others	14

In all, the SAR crews attended 2,017 incidents during 1992 and assisted 1,353 people in distress.

Mountain Rescue

The final link in the SAR chain is provided by the six Mountain Rescue teams covering the mountainous areas of the United Kingdom. Each team comprising about 30 men is equipped with suitable vehicles and a comprehensive range of climbing and rescue equipment. The men are all highly dedicated, and give up large amounts of their spare time for training. As a result, each team is made up of highly skilled mountaineers who know their local area very well, and are on one hour's notice all year round. Often they work with the SAR helicopters to successfully conclude what would be an impossible task for a helicopter alone, particularly in bad weather. Mountain rescue teams are based at Kinloss (29), Leuchars (30), Valley (19), Leeming (11), Stafford (17) and St Athan (19). Figures in Brackets refer to call outs during 1992.

Medical Support

The Royal Air Force Nursing Service was formed on June 1, 1918, and by the end of that year, numbered 42 nursing sisters, who although they held officer status were known by their professional titles. In June 1923, King George V gave the Royal Assent for the RAF Nursing Service to be known as Princess Mary's Royal Air Force Nursing Service (PMRAFNS).

With the outbreak of hostilities in 1939, the Service was enlarged and during the Second World War, the nursing sisters served in every operational theatre in static and mobile hospitals, in the sick bays of troop ships, in casualty reception areas and played their part in casualty evacuation flights. After the war casualty air evacuation, renamed aeromedical evacuation, was further developed and members of the PMRAFNS participated in the evacuation of casualities from areas such as Korea, Malaya, Borneo, Aden, Cyprus, Falkland Islands and the Gulf.

Currently there are three methods of entry: as Commissioned Officers, Staff Nurses, and Enrolled Nurses. All entrants to the PMRAFNS must be registered with the United Kingdom Central Council for Nursing Midwifery and Health Visiting. PMRAFNS is fully integrated in the Royal Air Force. Nursing Officers hold the Queen's Commission, use rank titles and complete either Short Service Commissions or enjoy a full career with a Permanent Commission. Non-commissioned ranks enter on variable time engagements with opportunities for career development and promotion.

Today members of the PMRAFNS serve at RAF Hospitals and Medical Centres at home and overseas. In the UK, mainly at the RAF Hospitals Halton & Wroughton and the Defence Rehabilitation Centre at Headley Court. Overseas at the RAF Hospitals at Wegberg in Germany and at Akrotiri in Cyprus.

Some indication of the workload of an RAF Hospital can be obtained from recent figures published for RAF Hospital Halton.

	1990	1991	1992
Service Patients	13,175	10,899	7,278
Civilian Patients	37,121	12,599	5,578
Available Beds	141	127	158

During FY 1992/93, the RAF spent £5.61 million on drugs and dressings. During the same period, the Army spent £12.19 million and the Royal Navy £3.29 million.

Medical Officers and dentists are recruited from civilian life having gained the relevant professional qualification. Figures for RAF uniformed medical personnel (At 1 Apr 1993) were:

Doctors	368
Dentists	119
Nurses	2,038 (Figure includes males, females and support staff).

RAF Regiment

The need to raise a dedicated specialist force to protect air installations became apparent during WWII when unprotected aircraft on the ground were vulnerable to enemy air and ground attack. Consequently, the RAF Regiment was raised on 1 February 1942 by a Royal Warrant of King George VI. At the end of WWII, there were over 85,000 personnel serving in the RAF Regiment manning 240 operational squadrons. During late 1993, the strength of the RAF Regiment is approximately 3,000 (including 264 officers). Following restructuring, strength is believed to be planned to be at about 2,400 by mid 1995.

Currently the RAF Regiment exists to provide ground and short range air defence for RAF installations, and to train all of the RAF's combatant personnel to enable them to contribute to the defence of their units.

As of 1 April 1994 RAF Regiment units are as follows:

No 1 Group (STC)

No 2 Squadron	Honnington	Field Squadron
No 3 Squadron	Aldergrove	Field Squadron

No 2 Group (STC)

No 1 Squadron	Laarbruch	Field Squadron
No 26 Squadron	Laarbruch	Rapier
No 37 Squadron	Bruggen	Rapier

No 11 Group (STC)

No 15 Squadron	Leeming	Rapier
No 27 Squadron	Leuchars	Rapier
No 48 Squadron	Lossiemouth	Rapier

British Forces Cyprus (STC)

No 34 Squadron	Akrotiri	Field Squadron

No 6 Wing (STC) (For deployment in support of USAF)

No 19 Squadron	Brize Norton	Rapier
No 20 Squadron	Honnington	Rapier
No 66 Squadron	Honnington	Rapier

Independent STC Units

No 63 (QCS)	Uxbridge	Ceremonial/Field Squadron

PTC Units

RAF Regiment Depot	Honnington
Rapier Training Unit	Honnington

Specialist RAF Regiment training for gunners is given at the RAF Regiment Depot at Honnington. On completion of training at the RAF College Cranwell officers also undergo further specialist training at RAF Honnington, and in some cases the

103

School of Infantry at Warminster in Wiltshire or the Royal School of Artillery at Larkhill. The RAF Regiment also mans the Queen's Colour Squadron which undertakes all major ceremonial duties for the Royal Air Force. These duties involve mounting the Guard at Buckingham Palace on an occasional basis, and providing Guards of Honour for visiting Heads of State. The Queen's Colour Squadron also has a war role as a field squadron.

The regiment is not alone in defending any RAF station. Every airman based at a station has a ground defence role and is trained to defend his place of work against ground attack and attack by NBC weapons. Training for this is given by RAF Regiment instructors who provide courses at station level on various aspects of ground defence for all personnel.

There are now two basic RAF Regiment squadron organisations - the field squadron organised for ground defence against possible enemy ground action and the rapier squadron organised for defence against low-flying enemy aircraft. There are four dedicated field squadrons and 63 (QCS) Squadron with a dual ceremonial/field squadron role. Five rapier squadrons defend RAF airbases and three rapier squadrons have a role in defending USAF bases in the UK.

Rapier Squadron-Possible Organisation

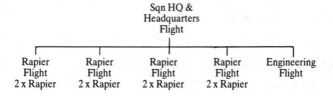

Rapier Characteristics

Guidance Semi Automatic to Command Line of Sight (SACLOS); Missile Diameter 13.3 cm; Missile Length 2.35m; Rocket Solid Fuelled; Warhead High Explosive; Launch Weight 42kg; Speed Mach 2+; Ceiling 3,000m; Maximum Range 6,800m; Fire Unit Height 2.13m; Fire Unit Weight 1,227kg; Radar Height (in action) 3.37m; Radar Weight 1,186kg; Optical Tracker Height 1.54m; Optical Tracker Weight 119kg; Generator Weight 243kg; Generator Height 0.91m.

The Rapier system provides area, Low Level Air Defence (LLAD) over the area around the airbase to be defended. It consists of an Optical Tracker, a Fire Unit, a Radar and a Generator. The into-action time of the system is thought to be about 15 minutes and the radar is believed to scan out to 12km. Each fire unit can therefore cover an Air Defence Area (ADA) of about 100 square kms. Having discharged the 4 missiles on a Fire Unit, 2 men are thought to be able to carry out a reload in about 3 minutes.

During the Falklands Campaign, Rapier was credited with 14 kills and 6 probables from a total of 24 missiles fired.

We believe that Rapier in service with the RAF Regiment are Field Standard B1(M) and that these equipments will be ugraded to Field Standard C (Rapier 2000).

Rapier FSC will offer significant enhancements to performance.

The towed system launcher will mount eight missiles (able to fire two simultaneously at 2 separate targets) which will be manufactured in two warhead versions. One of these warheads will be armour piercing to deal with fixed wing targets, and the other a fragmentation warhead for the engagement of cruise missiles and RPVs. Rapier 2000 will have the Darkfire tracker and a tailor made 3-dimensional radar system for target acquisition developed by Plessey.

A Joint Service Rapier FSC OCU has formed at RAF Honnington to oversee both the RAF's and Army's conversion to the new system. No 48 Sqn at RAF Lossiemouth is planned to be the first unit to convert to Rapier FSC in 1994 and the final squadron conversion should take place in 1995.

Rapier has now been sold to the armed forces of at least 14 nations. We believe that sales have amounted to over 25,000 missiles, 600 launchers and 350 Blindfire radars.

During June 1993 the UK MOD announced a reorganisation of the reserve forces and that by 1997, about 50% of the complement of No 15 Squadron (RAF Leeming) and No 27 Squadron (RAF Leuchars), both equipped with Rapier, would be members of the Royal Auxiliary Air Force Regiment.

Royal Auxiliary Air Force Regiment (RAuxAF Regt)

Airfield defence is further enhanced by squadrons of the RAuxAF Regt who are recruited locally and whose role is the ground defence of the airfield and its associated outlying installations. A RAuxAF Regt Sqn has an all up strength of about 120men and costs approximately £500,000 a year to keep in service. As a general rule, a squadron has a headquarters flight, two mobile flights mounted in Land Rovers and two flights for static guard duties. RAuxAF Regt squadrons are as follows:

1310 Wing RAuxAF Regt	RAF Honnington	HQ Unit
2503 Sqn RAuxAF Regt	RAF Waddington	Ground Defence
2620 Sqn RAuxAF Regt	RAF Marham	Ground Defence
2622 Sqn RAuxAF Regt	RAF Lossiemouth	Ground Defence

2624 Sqn RAuxAF Regt	RAF Brize Norton	Ground Defence
2625 Sqn RAuxAF Regt	RAF St Mawgan	Ground Defence
2729 Sqn RAuxAF Regt	RAF Waddington	Ground Defence
2890 Sqn RAuxAF Regt	RAF Waddington	Ground Defence

RAF Reserves

The reserve component of the Royal Air Force in late 1993 was as follows:

RAuxAF & RAFVR Reserves	-	2,200
Reserve Officers	-	600
Class E Airmen/Airwomen	-	11,000
Airmen Pensioners	-	22,000
Officer Pensioners	-	8,000
Total		**43,800**

* Aircrew who have served on Short Service Commissions have a mandatory reserve liability of four years.

The Controller Reserve Forces (RAF) is located at RAF Innsworth as part of RAF PTC. He is responsible for all of the non operational aspects of reserve forces policy and co-ordination, ranging from recruitment, through training, promotions and welfare to future planning. The following are the formed Reserve Units (RAuxAF Regt Squadrons are listed in the preceeding RAF Regiment section).

Royal Auxiliary Air Force

No 1 Maritime HQ	Northwood (London)
No 2 Maritime HQ	Pitrivie (Scotland)
No 3 Maritime HQ	RAF St Mawgan
4624 Movements Sqn	RAF Brize Norton Air Movements
4626 Aeromedical Evacuation Sqn	RAF Hullavington

Royal Auxiliary Air Force Defence Force Flights

RAuxAF Defence Force Flight (Brampton)
RAuxAF Defence Force Flight (High Wycombe)
RAuxAF Defence Force Flight (Lyneham)
RAuxAF Defence Force Flight (St Athan)

Royal Air Force Volunteer Reserve

7000 Flight, Royal Air Force Volunteer Reserve
7010 Flight, Royal Air Force Volunteer Reserve
7630 Flight, Royal Air Force Volunteer Reserve
7644 Flight, Royal Air Force Volunteer Reserve

In war, these four flights would provide specialist assistance in public relations, foreign language interrogation, photographic interpretation and intelligence support.

Royal Air Force Volunteer Reserve - Airman Aircrew Augmentation

    120 Sqn   -   Kinloss
    201 Sqn   -   Kinloss

This programme covers a number of air electronics operators who fly either Nimrod aircraft on maritime patrol.

Note: There are currently believed to be approximately 2,000 posts with the RAuxAF and a further 200 with the RAFVR. Proposals have been announced (1993) by the MOD for both of these organisations to be amalgamated, producing a more streamlined organisation for war.

RAF Police

The RAF Police exists to assist in protecting the operational assets and personnel of the RAF from the threats of espionage, sabotage, subversion, terrorism and crime. Headquarters of the RAF Provost and Security Services (P&SS) in the UK is at RAF Rudloe Manor. The basic organisation of HQ (P&SS)(UK) is as follows:

Vetting Wing - Responsible for the security vetting of all RAF Personnel, civilians employed by the Air Force Department and a variety of contractors. The majority of posts in this department have been civilianised.

Support Wing - Foward planning, budgets and co-ordination of P&SS world wide. Support Wing has the responsibility for operating the Police Logistic Information Data Management Information System (PLODMIS).

Operations Wing - Manages specialised tasks and co-ordinates activities of field units. Operations wing can provide a 55 man force to support P&SS operations world wide and provide security for the Air Transport force. In addition, a permanent standby for the Nuclear Accident Response Organisation is provided. Other specialist team include personnel who undertake key point security surveys and investigators who specialise in low flying complaints, operating Skyguard Radars to track and monitor RAF aircraft in low flying areas.

RAF Police detachments are to be found on almost all RAF stations. In the UK, they are responsible for security and policing inside RAF stations, and abroad in addition to having a responsibility for station security, act as the civilian police force for the services and their dependents.

Women's Royal Air Force (WRAF)

The Women's Royal Air Force came into existence in April 1, 1918, with elements of the Women's Auxiliary Army Corps and Women's Royal Naval Service already serving with the air units of the Army and Navy being offered a transfer to the new Service. During its brief two-year life, the WRAF boasted 32,000 members, until it was disbanded in 1920. It was then reformed in 1938 prior to the outbreak of WWII. By mid-1943, nearly 182,000 women were serving in 22 officer branches and 75 trades.

There are now very few branches of trade groups which are not open to women. Women enjoy equal rights in pay and employment with their male counterparts and are found working alongside them in key positions.
Many developments have taken place since 1949 reflecting changes in recruiting policy. The most significant in recent years was the decision, in 1989, to allow women to become pilots and navigators with the RAF. As of 19 Oct 93, there 8 x female pilots with a further 17 trained navigators. A further 21 pilots and 6 navigators were undergoing training.

On the 1st April 1994, the WRAF was disbanded and personnel integrated into the RAF "to eliminate any possible artificial barrier to further integration". In taking this step the RAF falls into line with the other two services who have already disbanded the WRNS and the WRAC.

"There are only two types of air station in both countries - good ones and bad ones. This is a good one".

Colonel Boris Krayushkin - Russian Air Force
During a CFE Treaty Inspection of RAF Coltishall in April 1993

Aberporth	-	Defence Research Agency
Abingdon	-	Now mainly for Army use
Alconbury	-	USAF - 95th Recce Sqn Withdraws in September 1995 (could remain a USAF enclave)
Aldergrove	-	72 Sqn - 15 x Wessex 230 Sqn - 15 x Puma 3 Sqn RAF Regiment Queens UAS - 4/5 x Bulldog 665 Sqn AAC - 17 x Gazelle AH-1 & 9 x Lynx AH-7 1 Flight AAC - 5 x Islander 13 AEF (Bulldogs from Queens UAS)
Ash	-	Radar Early Warning (CRC & Reserve SOC) Operational Conversion Unit
Bawdsey	-	Closure
Bedford	-	Defence Research Agency
Benbecula	-	Radar Early Warning (CRP & RP)
Benson	-	The Queens Flight - 3 x BAe 146 & 2 x Wessex Wessex Servicing Flight HQ Support Helicopter Force 115 Sqn - 7 x Andover (disbanding *) 60 Sqn - 9 x Wessex London UAS - 9/10 x Bulldog Oxford UAS - 4/5 x Bulldog 6 AEF - 4/5 Chipmunk T10 HQ No 1 Group Mobile Catering Support Unit

Note : * 115 Sqn is to be contractorised and the aircraft will be transferred to

Hunting Aviation's base at East Midlands Airport. Once civilian crews have been trained - 115 Sqn and the Andover Conversion Flight will disband. The RAF will remain in control of the aircraft's tasking.

Bently Priory	-	Headquarters No 11 Group UKADGE - System Development Centre Standby Air Defence Operations Centre (ADOC)
Bentwaters	-	USAF vacated September 1994 Probably due for closure
Biggin Hill	-	Closure
Binbrook	-	Future uncertain
Boddington	-	Communications Centre
A&EE Boscombe Down	-	Empire Test Pilots School Central Tactics and Trials Organisation (CTTO) Strike Attack Operational Evaluation Unit (SAOEU)
Boulmer	-	202 Sqn (SAR) - Sea King Radar Early Warning (CRC & RP + Reserve SOC) School of Fighter Control
Bracknell	-	RAF Staff College RAF Presentation Team Director Defence Studies
Brampton	-	Headquarters Logistic Command MOD Weapons Standardisation Team
Brawdy	-	USAF withdraws in September 1996 UK SOSUS terminal B Flight 202 Sqn withdraws 1 April 1994 Becomes an Army Facility
Brize Norton	-	10 Sqn - 10 x VC10 C1/C1K* 101 Sqn - 9 x VC10 K2/3 216 Sqn - 8 x Tristar K1/KC1/C2 55 Sqn (R) Ex 241 OCU No 1 Parachute Training School Air Transit Centre Tactical Communications Wing 4624 Movements Squadron R Aux AF

4624 Movements Squadron R Aux AF
2624 Sqn R Aux AF Regt
RAF Movements School
Air to Air Refueling (AAR) School
Joint Air Transport Establishment

(*10 Sqn generally have 8 x airframes and 17 flight crews available for operations at any one time).

Buchan	-	Radar Early Warning Control and Reporting Centre Sector Operations Centre
Burtonwood	-	Being vacated by USAF (Oct 1993)
Cardington	-	217 Maintenance Unit Cyrogenic & Compressed Gas Supply
Carlisle	-	No 14 Maintenance Unit (Closes 31 March 1997)
Caerwent	-	US Army Munitions Site (Closes December 1993)
Catterick	-	RAF Regiment Depot (Closes 1994) No 3 Wing RAF Regiment (Closes 1994) 645 VGS (Becomes an army facility)
Chilmark	-	For Closure in 1995 No 11 Maintenance Unit Chilmark Ammunition Depot
Chivenor	-	A Flight 22 Sqn (re-equipping with Sea King) 7 FTS 19 Sqn (R) - 25 x Hawk 92 Sqn (R) - 22 x Hawk 624 VGS

(Flying Training ceases 1 Oct 94 and station placed upon a care and maintenance basis from 1 Oct 95).

Church Fenton	-	Some areas closed - remains a relief landing ground for RAF Linton-on-Ouse
Colerne	-	Bristol UAS - 4/5 Bulldog

		3 AEF - 5 x Chipmunk
Coltishall	-	6 Sqn - 14 x Jaguar
		41 Sqn - 14 x Jaguar
		54 Sqn - 15 x Jaguar
		E Flight 22 Sqn - Wessex (Disbands June 1994)
		Jaguar Maintenance School
Conningsby	-	5 Sqn - 14 x Tornado F3
		29 Sqn - 14 x Tornado F3
		56 Sqn (R) - 21 x Tornado F3 (Tornado OCU)
		Battle of Britain Memorial Flight
Cosford	-	Birmingham UAS - 4/5 Bulldog
		RAF School of Technical Training
		633 VGS
		RAF School of Physical Training
Cottesmore	-	Trinational Tornado Trg Unit - 17 x Tornado GR1
Cranwell	-	The RAF College
		Dept of Initial Officer Trg (DIOT)
		Dept of Specialist Ground Training (DSGT)
		Dept of Air Warfare (DAW)
		3 FTS - Approx 60 x Tucano
		HQ University Air Squadrons
		Directorate of Recruiting & Selection
		Officers & Aircrew Selection Centre
		RAF College Band
Digby	-	Aerial Erector Training School
		399 Signals Unit
		591 Signals Unit
Elvington	-	Closed late 1992
Fairford	-	USAF Facility
Farnborough	-	Institute of Aviation Medicine
Finningley	-	6 FTS - 4 x Bulldog; 17 x Dominie T1; 8 x Hawk T1;
		10 x Tucano
		Air Navigation School
		Basic Navigation Wing (BNW)
		Advanced Navigation Wing (ANW)
		45 Sqn (R) - 11 x Jetstream (Part of 6FTS)
		Yorkshire UAS - 4/5 Bulldog

	-	9 AEF - 4/6 Chipmunk
		100 Sqn - 12 x Hawk (from Wyton late 1993)
		Air Loadmasters School
Fylingdales	-	Radar Early Warning
		AN/FPS-115 Radar
RAF(U) Goose Bay	-	Air Transit Base (approx 90 personnel)
Greenham Common	-	Site now for Sale
Halton	-	RAF Hospital
		612 VGS
		613 VGS
		No 1 School of Technical Training
		(moving to RAF Cosford)
		General Service Training Wing
		Recruit Training (from Swinderby)
		Airman's Command School
		Administration Training (from Hereford)
		RAF School of Catering
		RAF Police School (- Dog Training) from 1994
		RAF School of Education & Trg Support from 1994
Harrogate	-	Functions move to RAF Wyton 1994/95
Henlow	-	616 VGS
		Signals Engineering Establishment
		Radio Introduction Unit
		MOD Civilian Technical Training
		Test Equipment Engineering
		Officers Command School
		Air Cadets Regional HQ
Hereford	-	Closure by July 1994
High Wycombe	-	Headquarters Strike Command
		Central Tactics and Trials Organisation
		UK Region Air Operations Centre (UKRADOC)
		HQ 38 Group
		HQ AFNORTHWEST (From 1 July 1994)
Honnington	-	20 Sqn RAF Regiment
		RAF Regiment Depot (from Catterick in May 1994)
		HQ 6 Wing RAF Regt (from West Raynham in 1994)

		2 Sqn RAF Regt (from Catterick in 1994)
		16 Sqn RAF Regt - Rapier Training Unit (from West Raynham in 1994)
		Joint Service Rapier FSC (OCU)
		19 Sqn RAF Regt (from Brize Norton in 1994)
		1310 Wing R Aux AF Regt (from Catterick in 1994)
		13 Sqn - 13 x Tornado GR1A (Marham early 1994)
		(regular flying operations cease in mid 1994)
Hullavington	-	Closure March 1993
		Balloon Operations Squadron
		621 VGS - from late 1994
		Becomes an Army facility
Innsworth	-	RAF Personnel Management Centre
		HQ RAF Personnel & Training Command (1 April 94)
Jurby Head	-	Closed July 1993
Kemble	-	Army Vehicle Storage Site
Kinloss	-	Nimrod Main Servicing Unit
		120 Sqn - 7 x Nimrod MR2
		201 Sqn - 7 x Nimrod MR2
		206 Sqn - 7 x Nimrod MR2
		42 Sqn (R) - 5 x Nimrod (OCU)
		663 VGS

* There are believed to be 26 x Nimrod MR2 at Kinloss. For ease of reference we have shown them as being allocated to Sqns.

Lakenheath	-	USAF - 48th Fighter Wing
Leconfield	-	Army School of Mechanical Transport
		Flight 202 Sqn (SAR) Sea King
Leeming	-	11 Sqn - 17 x Tornado F3
		23 Sqn - 14 x Tornado F3 (disbands 1 Apr 94)
		25 Sqn - 17 x Tornado F3
		15 Sqn RAF Regiment - Rapier
		Northumbrian UAS - 4/5 Bulldog
		11 AEF - 4 x Chipmunk
		Mountain Rescue Team

Leuchars	-	43 Sqn - 15 x Tornado F3
		111 Sqn - 15 x Tornado F3
		27 Sqn RAF Regt - Rapier
		Aberdeen & St Andrews UAS - 4/5 Bulldog
		Mountain Rescue Team

| Lingholm | - | Communications Centre |

Linton-On-Ouse	-	No 1 Flying Training School - 22 x Tucano T1;
		17 x Bulldog T1.
		642 VGS
		Air Cadets Regional HQ

| Llanbedr | - | Defence Research Agency |

Locking	-	No 1 Radio School
		UKADGE - Engineering Training Facility
		Ground Communications Training
		RAF South West Band

Lossiemouth	-	12 Sqn - 13 x Tornado GR1
		208 Sqn - 13 x Buccaneer; 4 x Hunter*
		617 Sqn - 13 x Tornado GR1
		15 Sqn (R) - 21 x Tornado GR1 (TCWU)
		16 Sqn (R) - 15 x Jaguar (OCU)
		48 Sqn RAF Regiment - Rapier
		2622 Sqn R Aux AF Regt - Ground Defence
		D Flight 202 Sqn (SAR) Sea King

* 208 Sqn disbands on 1 April 1994.

Lyneham	-	24 Sqn - 13 x Hercules C1/C3/C1K
		30 Sqn - 13 x Hercules C1/C3/C1K
		47 Sqn - 11 x Hercules C1/C3/
		70 Sqn - 12 x Hercules
		57 Sqn (R) - 5 x Hercules
		Mobile Air Movements Sqn (MAMS)
		4626 R Aux AF Aeromedical Evacuation Sqn

Manston	-	C Flight 202 Sqn (To Wattisham June 1994)
		617 VGS- 5 x Viking TX1
		1 AEF - 5 x Chipmunk
		Defence Fire Services Training Establishment

Marham	-	2 Sqn - 13 x Tornado GR1A
		13 Sqn - 13 x Tornado GR1 (from Honnington 1994)
		39 (1 PRU) Sqn - 7 x Canberra (from Wyton late 1993)
		55 Sqn - 8 Victor K (Disbands Oct 93)
		2620 Sqn R Aux AF Regt - Ground Defence
Mildenhall	-	USAF - 100th Air Refueling Wing
Mount Batten	-	Closed late 1992
Molesworth	-	USAF Facility
		Joint Analysis Centre (JAC)
Neatishead	-	Radar Early Warning
		Control and Reporting Centre
		Sector Operations Centre
Newton	-	RAF School of Education
		Guided Weapons School
		Headquarters Air Cadets
		RAF School of Physical Training
		RAF Police School
		Joint Services Dog Training Wing
		East Midlands UAS - 5 x Bulldog
		7 AEF - 5 x Chipmunk
		(Reduces to an enclave by March 1995)
North Coates	-	Closure
North Luffenham	-	Prevention Development Centre
		Ground Radio Servicing Centre
		Support Command Signals Headquarters
		Rapier Repair Facility

(Closes 1 October 1996 - All avionics, communications and electronic equipment servicing transferred to RAF Sealand).

Northolt	-	Station Flight - 2 x Islander CC2
		32 Sqn - 12 x HS125; 5 x Andover; 4 x Gazelle.
		(Andovers withdrawn by 1 April 1994)
Oakhanger	-	1001 Signals Unit
		UK Military Spacecraft Control Centre

Odiham	-	7 Sqn - 12 x Chinook; 1 x Gazelle 33 Sqn - 12 x Puma 27 Sqn (R) - 4 x Chinook; 5 x Puma
Northwood	-	Headquarters No 18 Group
Pitreavie	-	AOC Scotland & Northern Ireland Rescue Co-ordination Centre (RCC) NATO Communications Site No 2 Maritime Headquarters
Portreath	-	Relief landing ground for St Mawgan Radar Early Warning (CRP & RP)
Quedgeley	-	No 7 Maintenance Unit (Closes 31 March 1998)
Rudloe Manor	-	Headquarters Provost and Security Services RAF Communications Centre No 6 Signals Unit P&SS Support Sqn Flying Complaints Flight
St Athan	-	AOC Wales Wales UAS - 5 x Bulldog Station Flight - 2 x Hawk No 4 School of Technical Training/Civilian Technical Training School VC10 Servicing Hangar Aircraft Storage Flight 634 VGS MT Driver Training Squadron Ground Defence School Repair & Salvage Squadron General Engineering Wing Aircraft Servicing Wing
St Mawgan	-	Sea King Training Unit 2625 Sqn R Aux AF Regt - Ground Defence No 3 Maritime HQ Joint Maritime Communications Centre (Operational in April 1995) SAR Helicopter Engineering Sqn
Sealand	-	631 VGS No 30 Maintenance Unit

		Civilian Technical Training Air Cadets Regional Headquarters Specialist Electronic Repair Unit (Activities transferred from North Luffenham by 1 October 1996).
Saxa Vord	-	Radar Early Warning (CRP & RP)
Scampton	-	Central Flying School - 22 x Tucano; 10 x Bulldog; 12 x Hawk; Trade Management Training School Red Arrows- 11 x Hawk Joint Arms Control Implementation Group Tucano Logistic Support
Shawbury	-	No 2 Flying Training School - 24 x Gazelle; 11 x Wessex Central Flying School Central Air Traffic Control School No 8 AEF - 4 x Chipmunk Aircraft Storage Flight
Spadeadam	-	Electronic Warfare Tactics Range
Stafford	-	No 16 Maintenance Unit Tactical Supply Wing
Stanbridge	-	RAF Supply Control Centre Joint Services Air Trooping Centre (reduced to an enclave in 1995)
Stanmore	-	Admin Unit
Staxton Wold	-	Radar Early Warning
Swanton Morely	-	611 VGS - 5 x Viking TX1 Central Servicing Development Establishment Maintenance Analysis & Computing Division Closure in 1995
Swinderby	-	Closure July 1993
Topcliffe	-	Detachment No 1 FTS
Turnhouse	-	East Lowlands UAS - 4 x Bulldog 12 AEF - 5 x Chipmunk Headquarters Air Cadets Scotland & N Ireland

	-	HQ Provost & Security Scotland No 2 Maritime Headquarters Unit, R Aux AF No 3 Flight AAC (V) - Gazelle HQ 76 Regt RE (V) - Airfield Damage Repair
TY Croes	-	Radar Early Warning (CRP)
Upavon	-	Closure August 1993 - Now an Army facility 622 VGS remains (Hercules from Lyneham OCU will continue to use the airfield)
Upper Heyford	-	USAF - 20th Fighter Wing Withdraws in December 1994
Uxbridge	-	Queens Colour Sqn - RAF Regiment (63 Sqn) RAF Music Services Central Band of the Royal Air Force Military Air Traffic Organisation (MATO) Management - Dispersed Units & Personnel
Valley	-	No 4 Flying Training School 74 Sqn (R) - 21 x Hawk 234 Sqn (R) - 20 x Hawk SAR Training Flight - Wessex C Flight 22 Sqn - Wessex (Sea King from 1996) Search & Rescue Training Unit (SARTU)
Waddington	-	8 Sqn - 7 x E-3D Sentry 51 Sqn - 3 x Nimrod R1 (from Wyton early 1995) Electronic Warfare Operational Support Establishment (EWOSE) - from Wyton late 1995 2729 Sqn R Aux AF Regt - Skyguard/Oerlikon 2890 Sqn R Aux AF Regt - Skyguard/Oerlikon 2503 Sqn R Aux AF Regt - Ground Defence
Wattisham	-	C Flight 202 Sqn - Sea King (from 1994) RAF Mobile Radar Reserve 3 Regiment Army Air Corps 4 Regiment Army Air Corps (from 1995)
Welford	-	Ammunition Depot - Future Uncertain
West Drayton	-	Closure of Domestic Areas March 1994 London Air Traffic Control Centre (remains) Air Defence Notification Centre (remains)

West Freugh	-	Defence Research Agency
West Raynham	-	For Closure Rapier Training Unit to Honnington in 1994
Wethersfield	-	Vacated by USAF (Standby Deployment Facility)
Wittering	-	1 Sqn - 14 x Harrier 20 Sqn (R) - Approx 30 Harrier (OCU) Armament Support Unit (RAFASUPU) EOD Sqn
Woodbridge	-	USAF vacated in September 1994 Probably due for closure
Woodvale	-	Liverpool UAS - 4/5 x Bulldog Manchester UAS - 4/5 x Bulldog
Wyton	-	39 Sqn (1PRU) - 7 Canberra (to Marham Dec 1993) 51 Sqn - 3 x Nimrod R1 (to Waddington early 1995) 100 Sqn - 12 x Hawks (to Finningley late 1993) 360 Sqn - 10 x Canberra (disbanding in Oct 1994 - role civilianised) Electronic Warfare Operational Support Establishment (EWOSE) - to Waddington late 1995

Note: By early 1995 all flying squadrons will have been withdrawn and Wyton/Brampton will become the headquarters of the new RAF Logistics Command.

RAF Stations Abroad

Akrotiri	-	84 Sqn - 5 x Wessex 34 Sqn RAF Regt - Ground Defence 12 Signals Unit (Episkopi)
Ascension	-	Staging Post for Falklands
Belize	-	1417 Flight - 3 x Harrier (disbands mid 1993) 1563 Flight - 4 x Puma (disbands late 1993)

Bruggen	-	9 Sqn - 13 x Tornado GR1
		14 Sqn - 13 x Tornado GR1
		17 Sqn - 13 x Tornado GR1
		31 Sqn - 13 x Tornado GR1
		37 Sqn RAF Regiment - Rapier
		Bruggen Air Terminal/Military Airhead
Gatow	-	Berlin Station Flight - 2 x Chipmunk
		Closing in 1995
		(Luftwaffe Museum moves from Hamburg)
Gibraltar	-	Jaguar Detachments
Gutersloh	-	Closed 1993
		1 Regt Army Air Corps
Laarbruch	-	3 Sqn - 13 x Harrier
		4 Sqn - 13 x Harrier
		18 Sqn - 5 x Chinook; 5 x Puma
		1 Sqn RAF Regt - Ground Defence
		26 Sqn RAF Regt - Rapier
Mount Pleasant	-	78 Sqn - Chinook & Sea King
		1435 Flight - Tornado F3
		1312 Flight - Hercules
		Radar Early Warning
		RAF Regiment Detachments
Wildenrath	-	Closure 1993
Sek Kong	-	28 Sqn - 8 x Wessex

RAF Hospitals

Princess Mary's RAF Hospital - Akrotiri
Princess Mary's RAF Hospital - Halton
Defence Medical Rehabilitation Centre - Headley Court
Princess Alexandra's RAF Hospital - Wroughton
RAF Hospital - Wegberg
Reserve Hospital - Nacton Hall

Note: USAF contingency wartime hospitals at Chessington, Kirknewton & Lanark have been returned to UK MOD control. Currently their future is uncertain.

Afterthought

"And then after a flight or two I was sent to start Hornchurch air station as a night flying anti-Zeppelin station. I landed there and the aerodrome consisted of a large field full of sheep, an infuriated farmer and a still more infuriated dog. So when we had cleared off the sheep and I'd appeased the farmer and been billeted on him, I formed a flight there which consisted of, amongst others Leefe Robinson - and when I was away on a four-day leave doing something much more dangerous, which was getting married, he went up and bagged the first Zeppelin."

Sir Arthur Harris

CHAPTER 11 - MISCELLANEOUS

RAF Rank Structure

Officers

Marshal of the RAF	-	4 Medium Bands & 1 Thick Band
Air Chief Marshal	-	3 Medium Bands & 1 Thick Band
Air Marshal	-	2 Medium Bands & 1 Thick Band
Air Vice Marshal	-	1 Medium Band & 1 Thick Band
Air Commodore	-	1 Thick Band
Group Captain	-	4 Medium Bands
Wing Commander	-	3 Medium Bands
Squadron Leader	-	2 Medium & 1 Thin Band
Flight Lieutenant	-	2 Medium Bands
Flying Officer	-	1 Medium Band
Pilot Officer	-	1 Thin Band

List 1 Trades

Warrant Officer	-	Royal Coat of Arms
Flight Sergeant	-	Crown & Three Chevrons
Chief Technician	-	Three Chevrons & a 4 Bladed Propeller
Sergeant	-	Three Chevrons
Corporal	-	Two Chevrons
Junior Technician	-	4 Bladed Propeller

List 2 Trades

Warrant Officer	-	Royal Coat of Arms
Flight Sergeant	-	Crown & Three Chevrons
Sergeant	-	Three Chevrons
Corporal	-	Two Chevrons
Senior Aircraftman	-	Three Bladed Propeller
Leading Aircraftman	-	Two Bladed Propeller

Codewords and Nicknames

A Codeword is a single word used to provide security cover for reference to a particular classified matter, eg "Corporate" was the Codeword for the recovery of the Falklands in 1982. In 1990 "Granby" was used to refer to operations in the Gulf. A Nickname consists of two words and may be used for reference to an unclassified matter, eg "Lean Look" referred to an investigation into MOD organisations to identify savings in manpower.

Aircraft Accidents 1 Jan 1992 - 1 Jan 1993

Date	Aircraft	Service	Killed	Serious Injury
15 Feb	Hunter	RN	0	1
12 May	Lynx	Army	0	0
12 May	Tucano	RAF	0	0
14 May	Harrier	RAF	0	1
21 May	Puma	RAF	0	0
28 May	Sea Harrier	RN	0	0
9 Jul	Buccaneer	RAF	2	0
7 Aug	Harrier	RAF	0	0
22 Sep	Sea King	RAF	0	0
30 Sep	Hawk	RAF	1	0
16 Oct	Bulldog	RAF	1	1
26 Nov	Puma	RAF	4	0*
26 Nov	Gazelle	Army	0	2*
30 Nov	Gazelle	Army	0	0
15 Dec	Gazelle	Army	0	0

* In a mid air collision in South Armagh.

Army Air Corps

The Army obtains its aviation support from the Army Air Corps (AAC). The AAC is an independent organisation within the military structure having 5 separate regiments and a number of independent squadrons. The AAC also provides support for Northern Ireland on a mixed resident and roulement basis and the two squadrons concerned are sometimes referred to as the sixth AAC Regiment, although the units would disperse on mobilisation and have no regimental title. By the end of 1994 following the "Options for Change" restructuring AAC regimental locations will be as follows:

1 Regiment	-	Germany
3 Regiment	-	Wattisham
4 Regiment	-	Wattisham
9 Regiment	-	Dishforth
7 Regiment	-	Netheravon

In addition to the Regiments in the UK and Germany there are small flights in Cyprus, Suffield (Canada) and the Falklands Islands. In Hong Kong 660 Sqn has 10 aircraft with a small detachment in Brunei.

The AAC Centre at Middle Wallop in Hampshire acts as a focal point for all Army Aviation, and it is here that the majority of training for pilots and aircrew is carried out.

Although the AAC operates some fixed wing aircraft for training, liaison flying and radar duties, the main effort goes into providing helicopter support for the ground forces. About 300 AAC helicopters are used for antitank operations, artillery fire control, reconnaissance, liaison flying and a limited troop lift.

AAC Regimental Organisation

Organisations for the individual AAC Regiments are in a state of flux. The following wiring diagram outlines the organisation of a Divisional AAC Regiment tasked with operations on the Forward Edge of the Battle Area (FEBA). Various regimental organisations are a variation on this theme.

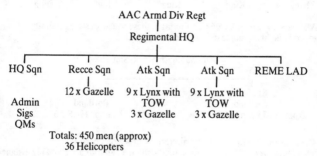

(1) A Regiment in an area where there is a high perceived armoured threat may have 3 x Antitank Squadrons.

Fleet Air Arm

The Fleet Air Arm provides the air support for the Royal Navy and the Royal Marines. Harrier Squadrons embark on the three carriers HMS Ark Royal, HMS Illustrious and HMS Invincible, as do detachments of the airborne early warning and anti submarine Sea King helicopter squadrons. The majority of RN ships of the destroyer/frigate type have their own anti submarine/anti ship Lynx aircraft that also serve a vital fleet communications role. Whilst not strictly part of the Fleet Air Arm, the Royal Marines 3 Cdo Bde Air Sqn is a Royal Naval organisation that provides communications and anti tank helicopter support for Commando forces operating ashore. The overall current Fleet Air Arm basic structure is as follows:

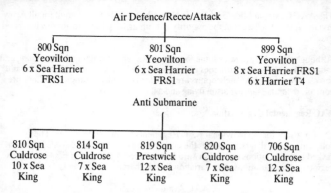

Air Defence/Recce/Attack

800 Sqn	801 Sqn	899 Sqn
Yeovilton	Yeovilton	Yeovilton
6 x Sea Harrier	6 x Sea Harrier	8 x Sea Harrier FRS1
FRS1	FRS1	6 x Harrier T4

Anti Submarine

810 Sqn	814 Sqn	819 Sqn	820 Sqn	706 Sqn
Culdrose	Culdrose	Prestwick	Culdrose	Culdrose
10 x Sea	7 x Sea	12 x Sea	7 x Sea	12 x Sea
King	King	King	King	King

(1) All Sea Kings are HAS 5/6 and aircraft in these squadrons are generally deployed in flights of single or multiple aircraft.

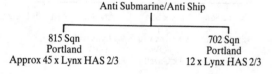

Anti Submarine/Anti Ship

815 Sqn	702 Sqn
Portland	Portland
Approx 45 x Lynx HAS 2/3	12 x Lynx HAS 2/3

(1) The majority of 815 Squadron's aircraft are at sea on board RN Frigates/Destroyers. Of the squadron total - about 30 aircraft are probably assigned to ships at any one time.

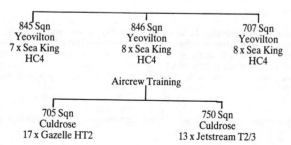

Commando Air Assault

845 Sqn	846 Sqn	707 Sqn
Yeovilton	Yeovilton	Yeovilton
7 x Sea King	8 x Sea King	8 x Sea King
HC4	HC4	HC4

Aircrew Training

705 Sqn	750 Sqn
Culdrose	Culdrose
17 x Gazelle HT2	13 x Jetstream T2/3

In addition to the above the Fleet Air Arm has the following:-

Airborne Early Warning	849 Sqn	Culdrose	8 x Sea King AEW2
Fleet Support & SAR	771 Sqn	Culdrose	5 x Sea King Mk5
	772 Sqn	Portland	6 x Sea King Mk4
Fleet Training & Support		Yeovilton	13 x Hunter T8/G11
3 Cdo Bde Air Sqn		Yeovilton	7 x Gazelle/ 6 x Lynx

Dates and Timings

When referring to timings the RAF uses the 24 hour clock. This means that 2015 hours, pronounced twenty fifteen hours, is in fact 8.15pm. The RAF usually avoids midnight and refer to 2359 or 0001 hours. Time zones present plenty of scope for confusion! Exercise and Operational times are expressed in Greenwich Mean Time (GMT) which may differ from the local time. The suffix Z (Zulu) denotes GMT and A (Alpha) GMT + 1 hour. B (Bravo) means GMT + 2 hours and so on.

The Date Time Group or DTG can be seen on RAF documents and is a point of further confusion for many. Using the DTG 1030 GMT on 20th April 1994 is written as 201030Z APR 94. When the RAF relates days and hours to operations a simple system is used:

a. D Day is the day an operation begins.
b H Hour is the hour a specific operation begins.
c. Days and hours can be represented by numbers plus or minus of D Day. Therefore if D Day is the 20th April 1991, D-2 is the 18th April and D + 2 is the 22nd April. If H Hour is 0600hrs then H+2 is 0800 hours.

Flying Hour

British military aircraft record flying time as being from the moment an aircraft takes off to the moment it lands, as opposed to commercial aircraft where flight time includes the time the aircraft taxies for departure and arrival.

Royal Air Force Rates of Pay as at 1st Jan 1995 (£ per day)

Officers	On Appointment	Rising To
University Cadet	20.45	26.35
Officer Cadet	24.98	-
Pilot Officer	35.59	-
Flying Officer	47.04	52.00
Flight Lieutenant	60.07	69.79
Squadron Leader	76.24	91.28

Wing Commander	107.33	118.61
Group Captain	124.97	138.13
Air Commodore	153.31	-

Notes:

(1) Rates of pay apply to both male and female officers.
(2) There are slightly different rates of pay for Branch Officers, Chaplains, Education Specialists, Medical Technicians and Directors of Music.

Airmen/Airwomen (Aircrew/Ground Trades & PMRAFNS) as at 1 Jan 95

	Band	Scale C (£ per day)
Aircraftman	1	23.03
Leading Aircraftman	1	25.71
Leading Aircraftman	2	29.73
Leading Aircraftman	3	34.56
Senior Aircraftman	1	31.10
Senior Aircraftman	2	35.14
Senior Aircraftman	3	39.60
Junior Technician	1	35.63
Junior Technician	2	39.68
Junior Technician	3	44.51
Corporal	1	40.47 (And ALM Cadets after satisfactory
Corporal	2	44.51 completion of Phase 1 Training)
Corporal	3	49.84
Sergeant	4	45.10
Sergeant	5	49.51
Sergeant	6	54.33
Chief Technician	4	47.16
Chief Technician	5	51.57
Chief Technician	6	56.38
Chief Technician	7	62.22
Flight Sergeant	4	49.23
Flight Sergeant	5	53.63
Flight Sergeant	6	59.00
Flight Sergeant	7	64.89
Warrant Officer & MACR	4	54.23
Warrant Officer & MACR	5	58.63
Warrant Officer & MACR	6	64.66
Warrant Officer & MACR	7	70.60

(1) Pay scales apply to both males and females.

(2) These rates only show the most common basic pay rates.

(3) There are three basic scales. Scale A (less than 6 years service); Scale B (6 years but less than 9 years); Scale C (9 years or more). The above table relates to scale C rates.

(4) After 9 years service personnel are eligible for extra daily long service increments of pay. These vary according to rank. For example a Corporal will get £1.10 per day extra after 12 years service and a Flight Sergeant £1.35 per day extra after 12 years service. Increments are awarded at the 9,12,15,18 & 22 year points.

(5) From the 1st January 1991 all recruits are enlisted on an Open Engagement. The Open Engagement is for a period of 22 years service from the age of 18 or the date of enlistment whichever is the later. Subject to giving 12 months notice, and any time bar that may be in force, all personnel have the right to leave on the completion of 3 years reckonable service from the age of 18.

RAF Flying Pay

Officer Aircrew

	£ per day
Initial Rate	8.86
Middle Rate	14.88
Top Rate	22.48
Wing Commander (after 6 years)	21.27
Wing Commander (after 8 years)	20.02
Group Captain	18.76
Group Captain (after 2 years)	17.50
Group Captain (after 4 years)	16.26
Group Captain (after 6 years)	14.40
Group Captain (after 8 years)	12.51

Specialist Aircrew Flight Lieutenants

On Appointment	28.93
After 1 Year	29.37
After 2 Years	29.81
After 3 Years	30.25
After 4 Years	30.69
Rises Annually - Until after 16 Years	36.47

Airman Aircrew

Lower Rate	4.39
Middle Rate	9.68
Top Rate	11.38

Miscellaneous Allowances

Parachutists Pay	3.35
Parachute Jumping Instructor's Pay	4.45
Aeromedical & Escort Duty	4.96
Diving Pay (RAF Diver)	2.55
Pay of an Objectionable Nature (Basic)	2.20
(Higher Rate)	11.15
Work in Unpleasant Conditions	0.60
Experimental Pay	1.70
Northern Ireland Pay	4.00
Separation Allowance (UK & NW Europe)	2.85
(Outside NW Europe)	3.65

Phonetic Alphabet

To ensure minimum confusion during radio or telephone conversations difficult
words or names are spelt out letter by letter using the following NATO standard
phonetic alphabet.

ALPHA - BRAVO - CHARLIE - DELTA - ECHO - FOXTROT - GOLF -
HOTEL-INDIA - JULIET - KILO - LIMA - MIKE - NOVEMBER - OSCAR -
PAPA-QUEBEC - ROMEO - SIERRA - TANGO - UNIFORM - VICTOR -
WHISKEY - X RAY - YANKEE - ZULU.

3(UK) Division Organisation

The major military organisation stationed in the United Kingdom is the 3rd (UK)
Division. The following is a guide to the organisation of this formation, that in war
would reinforce the ARRC or could be deployed to operational areas outside of the
NATO theatre of operations.

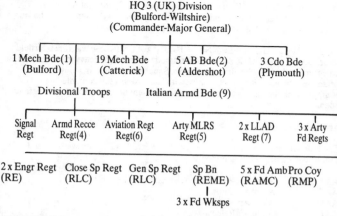

HQ 3 (UK) Division
(Bulford-Wiltshire)
(Commander-Major General)

| 1 Mech Bde(1) | 19 Mech Bde | 5 AB Bde(2) | 3 Cdo Bde |
| (Bulford) | (Catterick) | (Aldershot) | (Plymouth) |

Divisional Troops   Italian Armd Bde (9)

| Signal | Armd Recce | Aviation | Arty MLRS | 2 x LLAD | 3 x Arty |
| Regt | Regt(4) | Regt(6) | Regt(5) | Regt (7) | Fd Regts |

| 2 x Engr Regt | Close Sp Regt | Gen Sp Regt | Sp Bn | 5 x Fd Amb | Pro Coy |
| (RE) | (RLC) | (RLC) | (REME) | (RAMC) | (RMP) |

3 x Fd Wksps

3 (UK) Div Totals (excluding 3 Cdo Bde):
Main Battle Tanks (MBT) - Approx 100 x Challenger.
Armoured Infantry Fighting Vehicles (AIFV) - Approx 90 x Warrior
Armoured Personnel Carriers (APCs) - Approx 172 x Saxon.
Self Propelled (SP) Artillery - Approx 48 x AS90.
Lynx Helicopters armed with TOW missiles - approx 24

Note: (1) 1 Mechanised Brigade; (2) 5 Airborne Brigade; (3) 3 Commando Brigade
a Royal Naval formation is available to support 3(UK) Div if necessary.(4)
Armoured Reconnaissance Regiment; (5) Artillery Regiment with Multi Launch
Rocket System; (6) Army Air Corps Regiment with Lynx & Gazelle; (7) Air
Defence Regiments with Rapier and Javelin/Starstreak missiles;(8) The
composition of this division with a lightly armed parachute brigade plus a marine
commando brigade allows the UK MOD to retain a balanced force for out of
NATO area operations should that become necessary (9) Under Allied Rapid
Reaction Corps framework agreements this division could be reinforced by an
Italian Armoured Brigade (Ariete).

Airfield Damage Repair

The Army's Corps of Royal Engineers provide airfield damage repair (ADR) for
the RAF in both the UK and overseas. There are two organisations responsible for
this support. The first is the regular 39 Engineer Regiment, of whose three
squadrons one will provide support to RAF Bruggen, one to RAF Laarbruch and

the third to the RAF's UK airfields. The second is the Territorial Army's 73 Engineer Regiment, and this unit is available to provide ADR support to the Rapid Reaction Force (Air) as well as to the Main Defensive Forces.

Supported by 2 x Gazelles from No 2 FTS at Shawbury (whose war role is airfield recce/support) each ADR Squadron is trained to lay rolls of heavy matting over holes repaired with quick drying concrete. Squadron strength is about 100 personnel organised into three troops, with each troop a self contained unit, equipped with the plant and construction equipment necessary to keep an airfield open.

Abbreviations

The following is a selection from the list of standard NATO abbreviations and should assist users of this handbook.

A&AEE	Aeroplane & Armament Experimental Establishment
AAC	Army Air Corps
AAM	Air to Air Missile
AAR	Air to Air Refueling
ac	Aircraft
ACCGS	Air Cadets Central Gliding School
accn	Accommodation
ACE	Allied Command Europe
AD	Air Defence/Air Dispatch/Army Department
ADA	Air Defended Area
Adjt	Adjutant
admin	Administration
admin O	Administrative Order
ADOC	Air Defence Operations Centre
ADP	Automatic Data Processing
ADR	Airfield Damage Repair
ADV	Air Defence Variant
AEF	Air Experience Flight
AEW	Airborne Early Warning
AFCENT	Allied Forces Central European Theatre
Airmob	Airmobile
ALARM	Air Launched Anti Radiation Missile
ALM	Air Loadmaster
amn	airman
AMRAAM	Advanced Medium Range Air to Air Missile
AOC	Air Officer Commanding
ARRF	Allied Rapid Reaction Forces
ASRAAM	Advanced Short Range Air to Air Missile
ATAF	Allied Tactical Air Force
ATC	Air Traffic Control; Air Training Corps

Atk	Antitank
armr	Armour
armd	Armoured
AFV	Armoured Fighting Vehicle
AMF(L)	Allied Mobile Force (Land Element)
AMP	Air Member for Personnel
APC	Armoured Personnel Carrier
APDS	Armour Piercing Discarding Sabot
AP	Armour Piercing/Ammunition Point/Air Publication
ARRC	Allied Rapid Reaction Corps
ASF	Aircraft Servicing Flight
ATGW	Anti Tank Guided Weapon
att	Attached
AWOL	Absent Without Official Leave
BAe	British Aerospace
BALTAP	Baltic Approaches
BE	Belgium (Belgian)
BMEWS	Ballistic Missile Early Warning System
bde	Brigade
BAOR	British Army of the Rhine
BFG	British Forces Germany
BFPO	British Forces Post Office
BRSC	British Rear Support Command
cam	Camouflaged
cas	Casualty
CASEVAC	Casualty Evacuation
cat	Catering
CAD	Central Ammunition Depot
CAP	Combat Air Patrol
CATCS	Central Air Traffic Control School
CCTV	Closed Circuit Television
Cdo	Commando
CEP	Circular Error Probable
CEPS	Central European Pipeline System
CET	Combat Engineer Tractor
CINCENT	Commander in Chief Central European Theatre
CFE	Conventional Forces Europe
CFS	Central Flying School
COC	Combat Operations Centre
CoS	Chief of Staff
CRC	Control & Reporting Centre
CRP	Control & Reporting Post
CVD	Central Vehicle Depot
CW	Chemical Warfare
civ	Civilian
CP	Close Protection/Command Post

c sups	Combat Supplies
comd	Command/Commander
CinC	Commander in Chief
CPO	Command Pay Office/Chief Petty Officer
CO	Commanding Officer
comp rat	Composite Ration (Compo)
COMSEN	Communications Centre
coord	Co-ordinate
CCM	Counter Counter Measure
DAW	Department of Air Warfare
def	Defence
DF	Defensive Fire
DIOT	Director of Initial Officer Training (Cranwell)
DK	Denmark
dml	Demolition
det	Detached
div	Division
DRA	Defence Research Agency
DTG	Date Time Group
DS	Direct Support/Dressing Station
DSGT	Department of Specialist Ground Training
ech	Echelon
ECM	Electronic Counter Measure
ECCM	Electronic Counter Counter Measure
EFA	European Fighter Aircraft
EFTS	Elementary Flying Training Squadron
ELINT	Electronic Intelligence
emb	Embarkation
EDP	Emergency Defence Plan
EMP	Electro Magnetic Pulse
en	Enemy
engr	Engineer
EOD	Explosive Ordnance Disposal
eqpt	Equipment
ETA	Estimated Time of Arrival
ETPS	Empire Test Pilots School
EW	Early Warning/Electronic Warfare
ex	Exercise
FGA	Fighter Ground Attack
fmn	Formation
FAC	Forward Air Controller
FEBA	Forward Edge of the Battle Area
FLA	Future Large Aircraft
FLET	Forward Location Enemy Troops
FLIR	Forward Looking Infra Red
FLOT	Forward Location Own Troops

FOO	Forward Observation Officer
FR	France (French)
FRT	Forward Repair Team
FTS	Flying Training School
FY	Financial Year
GDP	General Defence Plan
GE	German (Germany)
GEF	Ground Equipment Flight
GR	Greece (Greek)
GOC	General Officer Commanding
GPMG	General Purpose Machine Gun
HAS	Hardened Aircraft Shelter
hel	Helicopter
HE	High Explosive
HEAT	High Explosive Anti Tank
HESH	High Explosive Squash Head
HVM	Hyper Velocity Missile
Hy	Heavy
IAM	Institute of Aviation Medicine
IFF	Identification Friend or Foe
IGB	Inner German Border
illum	illuminating
int	Intelligence
IO	Intelligence Officer
INTSUM	Intelligence Summary
IRG	Immediate Replenishment Group
IS	Internal Security
IT	Italy (Italian)
IUKADGE	Improved UK Air Defence Ground Environment
IW	Individual Weapon
JHQ	Joint Headquarters
JSSU	Joint Services Signals Unit
LC	Logistics Command
LGB	Laser Guided Bomb
L of C	Lines of Communication
LLAD	Low Level Air Defence
LO	Liaison Officer
Loc	Locating
log	Logistic
LRATGW	Long Range Anti Tank Guided Weapon
LSW	Light Support Weapon
MAOT	Mobile Air Operations Team
maint	Maintain
mat	Material
med	Medical
MNAD	Multi National Airmobile Division

MND	Multi National Division
MO	Medical Officer
MP	Military Police
MOD	Ministry of Defence
mob	Mobilisation
MovO	Movement Order
MPA	Mount Pleasant Airfield
MR	Maritime Reconnaissance
MRR	Maritime Radar Reconnaissance
MSAM	Medium Range Surface to Air Missile
msl	missile
MV	Military Vigilance
NAAFI	Navy, Army and Air Force Institutes
NADGE	NATO Air Defence Ground Environment
NATO	North Atlantic Treaty Organisation
NBC	Nuclear Biological and Chemical
NCO	Non Commissioned Officer
nec	Necessary
NL	Netherlands
NO	Norway (Norwegian)
NOK	Next of Kin
ni	Night
NORTHAG	Northern Army Group
NTR	Nothing to Report
NYK	Not Yet Known
OP	Observation Post
OC	Officer Commanding
OCU	Operational Conversion Unit
OEU	Operational Evaluation Unit
OIC	Officer in Charge
OLF	Operational Low Flying
opO	Operation Order
ORBAT	Order of Battle
pax	Passengers
POL	Petrol, Oil and Lubricants
P info	Public Information
PMRAFNS	Princess Mary's Royal Air Force Nursing Service
PO	Portugal (Portuguese)
PR	Public Relations
PRU	Photographic Reconnaissance Unit
PTC	Personnel & Training Command
QCS	Queen's Colour Squadron
QM	Quartermaster
QRA	Quick Reaction Alert
RAP	Rocket Assisted Projectile/Regimental Aid Post
RAuxAF	Royal Auxiliary Air Force

RIC	Reconnaissance Interpretation Centre
RP	Reporting Post
RPV	Remotely Piloted Vehicle
RTM	Ready to Move
R&D	Research and Development
rebro	Rebroadcast
recce	Reconnaissance
rft	Reinforcement
RTU	Return to Unit
SACEUR	Supreme Allied Commander Europe
SAM	Surface to Air Missile
SATCO	Senior Air Traffic Control Officer
SARTU	Search & Rescue Training Unit
2IC	Second in Command
SH	Support Helicopters
SHAPE	Supreme Headquarters Allied Powers Europe
SKTU	Sea King Training Unit
sit	Situation
SITREP	Situation Report
smk	Smoke
SMO	Senior Medical Officer
SNCO	Senior Non Commissioned Officer
SOC	Sector Operations Centre
SP	Spain (Spanish)
Sqn	Squadron
SSM	Surface to Surface Missile
SSR	Secondary Surveillance Radar
SSVC	Services Sound and Vision Corporation
STC	Strike Command
STOL	Short Take Off and Landing
tac	Tactical
TASM	Tactical Air to Surface Missile
tgt	Target
THAAD	Theatre High Altitude Area Defence
TOT	Time on Target
TOW	Tube Launched Optically Tracked Wire Guided Missile
tpt	Transport
TU	Turkish (Turkey)
TWCU	Tornado Weapons Conversion Unit
UAS	University Air Squadron
UK	United Kingdom
UKADGE	United Kingdom Air Defence Ground Environment
UKADR	United Kingdom Air Defence Region
UKRADOC	United Kingdom Region Air Defence Operations Centre
UKLF	United Kingdom Land Forces
UKMF	United Kingdom Mobile Force

UNCLASS	Unclassified
UNFICYP	United Nations Force in Cyprus
UXB	Unexploded Bomb
US	United States
USAF	United States Air Force
veh	Vehicle
VGS	Volunteer Gliding School
VOR	Vehicle off the Road
WE	War Establishment
wh	Wheeled
WIMP	Whinging Incompetent Malingering Person
WMR	War Maintenance Reserve
WO	Warrant Officer
WRNS	Womens Royal Naval Service
WRAC	Womens Royal Army Corps
WRAF	Womens Royal Air Force
wksp	Workshop
X	Crossing (as in roads or rivers)

ROYAL AIR FORCE

Planned Force Structure from 1 Jan 1995

Tornado F3	-	100 aircraft
Tornado GR1/1A/1B	-	112 aircraft (1)
Hawk	-	50 aircraft (2)
E-3D Sentry	-	6 aircraft
Harrier	-	52 aircraft
Jaguar	-	40 aircraft
Nimrod	-	27 aircraft
Support Helicopters	-	90 aircraft (3)(4)
Transport & Tanker Aircraft	-	90 aircraft

Notes:

(1) Excluding the aircraft at the Trinational Tornado Training Establishment. (2) Configured for the air defence role only. (3) There may be an increase in the numbers of support helicopters. A decision on EH101 or extra CH-47s is expected shortly. (4) Excludes SAR aircraft & Queens Flight.

This publication was produced by R&F (Defence) Publications.
The other publications in this series are:

The British Army Pocket Guide (Available early 1995)

Editorial Office 0743 - 235079

R&F (Defence Publications) has a consultancy arm that specialises
in all aspects of the United Kingdom and the European Union's
defence and security arrangements.

Further copies of this publication can be obtained from:

Pen & Sword Books Ltd
47 Church Street
Barnsley S70 2AS

Telephone: 0226 734222   Fax: 0226 734438
There are special rates for purchases of more than 10 books.